"This series is a tremendous resource for those v̱̱̱̱̱̱̱̱̱̱̱̱̱̱̱ ̱̱̱̱̱̱̱̱̱̱̱̱̱̱h an understanding of how the gospel is woven thṟ̱̱̱̱̱̱̱̱̱̱̱̱̱̱̱ ̱̱̱̱̱̱̱̱̱̱̱̱̱̱ded pastors and scholars doing gospel business froṉ̱̱̱̱̱̱̱̱̱̱̱̱̱ ̱̱̱̱̱̱̱̱̱̱̱̱̱̱̱eo-logical feast preparing God's people to apply the̱̱̱̱̱̱̱̱̱̱̱̱̱ ̱̱̱̱̱̱̱̱̱̱̱̱̱̱̱̱ind wholly committed to Christ's priorities."

BRYAN CHAPELL, President Emeritus, Co̱̱̱̱̱̱̱̱̱̱̱̱̱̱̱̱̱̱ ̱̱̱̱̱̱̱̱̱̱̱̱̱̱̱̱̱tor, Grace Presbyterian Church, Peoria, Illinois

"Mark Twain may have smiled when he wrote to a friend, 'I didn't have time to write you a short letter, so I wrote you a long letter.' But the truth of Twain's remark remains serious and universal, because well-reasoned, compact writing requires extra time and extra hard work. And this is what we have in the Crossway Bible study series *Knowing the Bible*. The skilled authors and notable editors provide the contours of each book of the Bible as well as the grand theological themes that bind them together as one Book. Here, in a 12-week format, are carefully wrought studies that will ignite the mind and the heart."

R. KENT HUGHES, Visiting Professor of Practical Theology, Westminster Theological Seminary

"*Knowing the Bible* brings together a gifted team of Bible teachers to produce a high-quality series of study guides. The coordinated focus of these materials is unique: biblical content, provocative questions, systematic theology, practical application, and the gospel story of God's grace presented all the way through Scripture."

PHILIP G. RYKEN, President, Wheaton College

"These *Knowing the Bible* volumes provide a significant and very welcome variation on the general run of inductive Bible studies. This series provides substantial instruction, as well as teaching through the very questions that are asked. *Knowing the Bible* then goes even further by showing how any given text links with the gospel, the whole Bible, and the formation of theology. I heartily endorse this orientation of individual books to the whole Bible and the gospel, and I applaud the demonstration that sound theology was not something invented later by Christians, but is right there in the pages of Scripture."

GRAEME L. GOLDSWORTHY, former lecturer, Moore Theological College; author, *According to Plan*, *Gospel and Kingdom*, *The Gospel in Revelation*, and *Gospel and Wisdom*

"What a gift to earnest, Bible-loving, Bible-searching believers! The organization and structure of the Bible study format presented through the *Knowing the Bible* series is so well conceived. Students of the Word are led to understand the content of passages through per-ceptive, guided questions, and they are given rich insights and application all along the way in the brief but illuminating sections that conclude each study. What potential growth in depth and breadth of understanding these studies offer! One can only pray that vast numbers of believers will discover more of God and the beauty of his Word through these rich studies."

BRUCE A. WARE, Professor of Christian Theology, The Southern Baptist Theological Seminary

KNOWING THE BIBLE

J. I. Packer, Theological Editor
Dane C. Ortlund, Series Editor
Lane T. Dennis, Executive Editor

•   •   •   •   •   •

Genesis	Psalms	Jonah, Micah, and Nahum	Ephesians
Exodus	Proverbs		Philippians
Leviticus	Ecclesiastes	Haggai, Zechariah, and Malachi	Colossians and Philemon
Numbers	Song of Solomon		
Deuteronomy	Isaiah	Matthew	1–2 Thessalonians
Joshua	Jeremiah	Mark	1–2 Timothy and Titus
Judges	Lamentations, Habakkuk, and Zephaniah	Luke	
Ruth and Esther		John	Hebrews
1–2 Samuel	Ezekiel	Acts	James
1–2 Kings	Daniel	Romans	1–2 Peter and Jude
1–2 Chronicles	Hosea	1 Corinthians	1–3 John
Ezra and Nehemiah	Joel, Amos, and Obadiah	2 Corinthians	Revelation
Job		Galatians	

•   •   •   •   •   •

J. I. PACKER was the former Board of Governors' Professor of Theology at Regent College (Vancouver, BC). Dr. Packer earned his DPhil at the University of Oxford. He is known and loved worldwide as the author of the best-selling book *Knowing God*, as well as many other titles on theology and the Christian life. He served as the General Editor of the ESV Bible and as the Theological Editor for the *ESV Study Bible*.

LANE T. DENNIS is CEO of Crossway, a not-for-profit publishing ministry. Dr. Dennis earned his PhD from Northwestern University. He is Chair of the ESV Bible Translation Oversight Committee and Executive Editor of the *ESV Study Bible*.

DANE C. ORTLUND (PhD, Wheaton College) serves as senior pastor of Naperville Presbyterian Church in Naperville, Illinois. He is an editor for the Knowing the Bible series and the Short Studies in Biblical Theology series, and is the author of several books, including *Gentle and Lowly: The Heart of Christ for Sinners and Sufferers*.

REVELATION

A 12-WEEK STUDY

Stephen Witmer

WHEATON, ILLINOIS

Knowing the Bible: Revelation, A 12-Week Study

Copyright © by Crossway

Published by Crossway
        1300 Crescent Street
        Wheaton, Illinois 60187

Some content used in this study guide has been adapted from the *ESV Study Bible*, copyright © 2008 by Crossway, pages 2453–2497. Used by permission. All rights reserved.

Cover design: Simplicated Studio

First printing 2015

Printed in the United States of America

All emphases in Scripture quotations have been added by the author.

Trade paperback ISBN: 978-1-4335-4320-3
EPub ISBN: 978-1-4335-4323-4
PDF ISBN: 978-1-4335-4321-0
Mobipocket ISBN: 978-1-4335-4322-7

Crossway is a publishing ministry of Good News Publishers.

VP		30	29	28	27	26	25	24	23
19	18	17	16	15	14	13	12	11	10	9

TABLE OF CONTENTS

SERIES PREFACE

KNOWING THE BIBLE, as the series title indicates, was created to help readers know and understand the meaning, the message, and the God of the Bible. Each volume in the series consists of 12 units that progressively take the reader through a clear, concise study of that book of the Bible. In this way, any given volume can fruitfully be used in a 12-week format either in group study, such as in a church-based context, or in individual study. Of course, these 12 studies could be completed in fewer or more than 12 weeks, as convenient, depending on the context in which they are used.

Each study unit gives an overview of the text at hand before digging into it with a series of questions for reflection or discussion. The unit then concludes by highlighting the gospel of grace in each passage ("Gospel Glimpses"), identifying whole-Bible themes that occur in the passage ("Whole-Bible Connections"), and pinpointing Christian doctrines that are affirmed in the passage ("Theological Soundings").

The final component to each unit is a section for reflecting on personal and practical implications from the passage at hand. The layout provides space for recording responses to the questions proposed, and we think readers need to do this to get the full benefit of the exercise. The series also includes definitions of key words. These definitions are indicated by a note number in the text and are found at the end of each chapter.

Lastly, for help in understanding the Bible in this deeper way, we urge readers to use the ESV Bible and the *ESV Study Bible*, which are available in various print and digital formats, including online editions at esv.org. The *Knowing the Bible* series is also available online.

May the Lord greatly bless your study as you seek to know him through knowing his Word.

J. I. Packer
Lane T. Dennis

WEEK 1: OVERVIEW

The book of Revelation is extraordinary in every way—not least in its hard-to-classify genre.[1] It is prophecy (1:3; 22:19) while also belonging to the genre of apocalyptic[2] writing (1:1), and it begins and ends with features that characterize the epistles of the New Testament (1:4–5; 22:21). Like other Jewish apocalypses, Revelation is filled with symbolic images from beginning to end. This allows for numerous possible interpretations of the book, and much diversity of opinion on matters such as the tribulation, the rapture, and the millennium.

Revelation begins with a vision of the resurrected and ascended Christ and his words to seven first-century churches in Asia Minor that were facing a range of challenges: persecution from without, false teaching from within, temptation to compromise with the surrounding pagan culture, and spiritual lethargy. The book then covers a vast sweep of time, from the first century all the way to the return of Christ.

Central to Revelation is its assertion that Christ has already won the victory over Satan through his death, and has therefore freed Christians from their sins by his blood (1:5). Christ's past, inaugurated (i.e., already begun) victory guarantees his future, consummated (i.e., fully completed) victory (2:26–27). Because Christ has already conquered Satan through his uniquely redemptive suffering, Christians can also "conquer" in the present by holding fast their witness in the face of enticing temptation or violent persecution, even if their faithful witness results in death.

Placing It in the Larger Story

Through its pervasive allusions to the Old Testament, Revelation demonstrates that Jesus Christ is the fulfillment and climax of history. Believers live after Jesus' first coming, suffering as he suffered, but full of hope because of his atoning death and their assurance of his future, victorious return. The entire book strains forward to the new heaven and new earth described in chapters 21–22.

Key Verse

"To him who loves us and has freed us from our sins by his blood and made us a kingdom, priests to his God and Father, to him be glory and dominion forever and ever. Amen." (Rev. 1:5b–6)

Date and Historical Background

Revelation was written by a man named John (1:1), most likely John the son of Zebedee, as suggested by early church tradition and indicated by links between Revelation and the Gospel of John (e.g., Jesus is the "Lamb" of God and the "Word" in both books). This is the John who was one of Jesus' original 12 disciples, and probably the one identified in John's Gospel as the disciple "whom Jesus loved" (John 13:23; 21:20). John likely wrote Revelation in the mid-90s AD, near the end of the reign of the Roman emperor Domitian, while in exile on the island of Patmos.

Outline

I. Prologue (1:1–8)

II. Substance (1:9–22:5)

    A. God's people imperfect in the world (1:9–3:22)

        1. The son of man among the lampstands (1:9–20)
        2. Seven letters to seven churches (2:1–3:22)

    B. The Lamb and the seven seals (4:1–8:1)

        1. The Lamb receives the scroll (4:1–5:14)
        2. The Lamb opens the seven seals (6:1–8:1)

    C. The seven angels and seven trumpets (8:2–11:19)

1. Prayers go up; fire comes down (8:2–5)
2. The seven trumpets are blown (8:6–11:19)

D. The cosmic conflict between Christ and Satan (12:1–14:20)

E. The seven angels and seven bowls (15:1–16:21)

1. Heaven's sanctuary is filled with glory (15:1–8)
2. The seven bowls are poured out (16:1–21)

F. The judgment of God's enemies (17:1–20:15)

1. Babylon, the beast, the false prophet (17:1–19:21)
2. Satan (20:1–10)
3. Unbelievers (20:11–15)

G. God's people perfect in glory (21:1–22:5)

III. Epilogue (22:6–21)

▶ As You Get Started . . .

When you think of the book of Revelation, what comes to mind? Do you think it refers mainly to events in the first century, events in our day, or events in the distant future?

Are you more intimidated or more intrigued by the colorful and often bizarre images throughout Revelation? Are there areas of confusion you hope will be cleared up through this study of Revelation?

Do you think of Revelation as a book mainly to be understood or to be obeyed, or both? Is it intended mainly to give us information, or to change our behavior, or both?

_____

_____

_____

_____

_____

_____

_____

▶ **As You Finish This Unit . . .**

As we'll see, God gives a blessing to every person who reads, hears, and obeys the words of Revelation (1:3). Take a moment to ask God for this special blessing, and for help in understanding this dazzling and mysterious book.

Definitions

[1] **Genre** – A type of literary work, characterized by a particular style, form, and content.

[2] **Apocalyptic** – The distinctive literary form of the book of Revelation and of chapters 7–12 of Daniel. These parts of Scripture include revelation about the future, highly symbolic imagery, and the underlying belief that God himself will one day end the world in its present form and establish his kingdom on a re-created earth.

Week 2: Prologue

Revelation 1:1–8

The Place of the Passage

The prologue of Revelation (1:1–8) sets the stage for the rest of the book. John shows that Revelation is not ultimately of human origin but comes from God. He also introduces some key terms ("who is and who was and who is to come," "witness") and themes (the death, resurrection, and return of Jesus) to which he will return throughout the book.

The Big Picture

Revelation 1:1–8 shows that the book of Revelation is of divine origin and is therefore a source of divine blessing for those who hear and obey it.

> ### Reflection and Discussion

Read through the complete passage for this study, Revelation 1:1–8. Then review
the shorter passages below and write your own notes on the following questions—
first with regard to the origin of Revelation (1:1–3) and then with regard to John's
greeting to the seven churches (1:4–8). (For further background, see the *ESV Study
Bible*, page 2463, or visit esv.org.)

1. The Origin of Revelation (1:1–3)

Verses 1–3 provide a six-part chain of revelation for the book of Revelation,
beginning with God and ending with the one who hears and keeps what is
written. Can you identify the four links of the chain in between? Why do you
think John begins the book with this chain of revelation?

Notice in verse 1 that some things "must" soon take place. Why do you think
John says they *must* take place? What does this suggest about his view of God?
Recalling that Revelation is written to suffering Christians, how would the
word "must" encourage them?

Jesus is the second link in the great chain of revelation. How does this uniquely
honor him?

How does John describe his relationship to Jesus in verse 1? Recalling that this is most likely John, the son of Zebedee, Jesus' best friend, how is John's self-description surprising? How does it bring glory to Jesus? What does it show us about John?

Verse 1 says that Jesus "made it known" to John. The Greek word for "make it known" indicates figurative representation, something that is made known by a sign. Moreover, in verse 2, John is to bear witness to all that he "saw." How does this prepare us to read the rest of Revelation? What does it lead us to expect about this book?

2. John's Greeting to the Seven Churches (1:4–8)

Verses 4–5a are a typical ancient letter address, following the normal form: "A to B, grace and peace" (compare Paul's letters). What is striking about this particular letter opening, though, is whom the grace and peace are *from*. Note that the Holy Spirit is pictured in verse 4 as seven spirits, representing fullness and perfection, since the Holy Spirit is active throughout the entire earth (see Rev. 5:6). In addition to the Holy Spirit, from whom do the grace and peace come? Why is this important? Why is it encouraging to the recipients of Revelation?

The book of Revelation calls for believers to be faithful witnesses in the face of persecution that may lead even to death (see Rev. 2:13). In light of that, how would the threefold description of Jesus in the first part of verse 5 encourage these believers?

How many comings of Jesus are mentioned in verses 5b–8? Note the two references to the cross. What do these verses tell us about what Jesus accomplished and will accomplish in these comings?

Read through the following three sections on *Gospel Glimpses, Whole-Bible Connections*, and *Theological Soundings*. Then take time to consider the *Personal Implications* these sections may have for you.

▶ Gospel Glimpses

GOD HAS A PLAN. For God's suffering people, the knowledge that God is in control and is unfolding his plan is unspeakably precious, hope-giving, and endurance-producing. So, the word "must" in verse 1 is important, because it demonstrates that God is sovereign over history. Events are happening purposefully, not randomly. Part of God's plan was the death of Jesus. The climax of the plan will be the glorious return of Jesus (1:7). God's sovereignty is a major theme of Revelation. His control over all things is praised in the song of the 24 elders in 4:11: "Worthy are you, our Lord and God, to receive glory and honor and power, for you created all things, and by your will they existed and were created." It is lauded too in the cry of 19:6: "Hallelujah! For the Lord our God the Almighty reigns."

DIVINE BLESSING. In 1:3, John pronounces a blessing on those who hear and keep the words of this book. The word "blessed" is the same word used by Jesus in the Beatitudes, and refers to receiving God's favor and provision. Verse 3 is the first of seven blessings throughout the book of Revelation. The penultimate of these seven blessings comes at the end of the book, in 22:7: "Blessed is the one who keeps the words of the prophecy of this book." Thus, 1:3 and 22:7 form "blessing bookends" for those who "keep" the words of the book. If we approach Revelation (as many do) simply to satisfy intellectual curiosity about end-time events, we'll miss the blessing it has for us. That blessing comes to those who hear God speaking, trust his plan, and obey his commands.

THE CROSS. The cross of Jesus is alluded to twice in these opening verses. In 1:7, John says Jesus was "pierced." In verse 5, he describes Jesus as the one who "freed us from our sins by his blood," shorthand for Jesus' death on the cross. Our sin had created a legal bondage of debt, and we owed God the penalty for it. Jesus freed us by paying our penalty on the cross.

▶ Whole-Bible Connections

JESUS THE ULTIMATE REVEALER. God revealed himself to his people throughout the Old Testament. He spoke to Adam and Eve in the garden (Genesis 2); to Moses in a burning bush (Exodus 3); to Israel in a thick cloud on top of Mount Sinai (Exodus 20); and repeatedly to his people through the Old Testament prophets (e.g., Jer. 1:1–10). The Gospel of John uniquely presents Jesus as the ultimate revealer of God, surpassing even Moses (John 1:17–18). Similarly, here in Revelation John claims that Jesus is the ultimate revealer of God and his plan. The whole book is, after all, "the revelation of Jesus Christ, which God gave him to show to his servants . . ." (Rev. 1:1). Jesus' role as the ultimate revealer is confirmed in Revelation 5, where only Jesus is worthy to open the scroll containing God's plan, and to break its seals. If Jesus is the ultimate revealer of God, one must know and accept Jesus in order to know God. This has major implications for how Christianity relates to the other world religions, which claim to know God but do not accept Jesus as being who he claimed to be.

A KINGDOM OF PRIESTS. Revelation 1:6 says Jesus makes believers "a kingdom, priests to his God and Father." John alludes here to the promise God gave through Moses in Exodus 19:6 that Israel would be "a kingdom of priests and a holy nation." Here John applies that promise not merely to God's people Israel, but to all Christians. Every Christian is part of God's kingdom and is a priest. As such, we all now offer worship to God, and will do so forever (Rev. 7:15).

We will see throughout Revelation that God's new covenant people in Christ (including Gentiles) inherit God's Old Testament promises to Israel.

Theological Soundings

REVELATION. According to 1:1, the book of Revelation is of divine rather than human origin (compare 22:16). Therefore, as God's word, it is not to be added to or altered in any way (22:18–19). This book embodies a very clear and high view of divine revelation.

THE TIME IS NEAR. The revelation of Jesus "must *soon* take place" (1:1) because "the time is near" (1:3). Interpreters differ on what exactly John is claiming here. Was he simply wrong (after all, it's been 2,000 years and counting)? Does he refer to the *certainty* of the events rather than to chronological imminence? Probably the best solution is to understand that the book of Revelation shares the viewpoint of the rest of the New Testament that the first coming of Jesus has already inaugurated (begun) the last days. Therefore, most of the eschatological[1] events prophesied throughout Revelation receive at least a beginning fulfillment in the period in which John is writing (and in our own day as well).

THE COMINGS OF GOD, FATHER AND SON. There's something unusual about the description of God in verse 4 and God's self-description in verse 8. We would expect God to be described as "him who is and who was and who *will be*." But instead, both verses say, "him who is and who was and who *is to come*." Why? The point of this description is not just that God will exist forever, but that he will *come* to judge and to save. At the very end of the book, in Revelation 22:12–13, we read: "Behold, I am coming soon, bringing my recompense with me, to repay each one for what he has done. I am the Alpha and the Omega, the first and the last, the beginning and the end." Here in verses 4–8, the announcement that God the Father will come again to this world is at the beginning (v. 4) and at the end (v. 8) of the section, forming a bracket around the paragraph. And strikingly, in between the two references to the coming of God the Father is a reference to the coming of *Jesus* (v. 7). God the Father will come in and through the coming of Jesus. This overlap between the comings of God the Father and Jesus points already to the deity of Jesus.

Personal Implications

Take time to reflect on the implications of Revelation 1:1–8 for your own life today. Make notes below on the personal implications for your walk with the Lord of the (1) *Gospel Glimpses*, (2) *Whole-Bible Connections*, (3) *Theological Soundings*, and (4) this passage as a whole.

1. Gospel Glimpses

2. Whole-Bible Connections

3. Theological Soundings

4. Revelation 1:1–8

As You Finish This Unit . . .

Take a moment now to ask for the Lord's blessing and help as you continue in this study of Revelation. And take a moment also to look back through this unit of study, to reflect on some key things that the Lord may be teaching you—and perhaps to highlight and underline these things to review again in the future.

Definitions

[1] **Eschatology** – Study of the end times as described in the Bible. Includes such topics as the return of Christ, the period of tribulation, the resurrection and judgment of all people, and the millennial reign of Christ on earth.

WEEK 3: GOD'S PEOPLE IMPERFECT IN THE WORLD

Revelation 1:9–3:22

The Place of the Passage

Having introduced his letter/apocalypse/prophecy (1:1–3), and having greeted the seven churches of Asia (1:4–8), John now reports his initial vision of the resurrected and exalted Christ (1:9–20) and records Christ's words to each of the seven churches (chs. 2–3). This opening section thus demonstrates the centrality of the risen Christ to the entire book, while also rooting the message of Revelation in the specific situations of suffering first-century churches (see also the phrase "for the churches" in 22:16).

The Big Picture

Revelation 1:9–3:22 shows that the exalted, all-powerful Christ knows the situations of his churches, however faithful and pressured they have been. He has not abandoned them but rather walks among them.

> ### Reflection and Discussion

Read through the complete passage for this study, Revelation 1:9–3:22. Then review the shorter passages below and write your own notes on the following questions. (For further background, see the *ESV Study Bible*, pages 2464–2469, or visit esv.org.)

1. The Son of Man among the Lampstands (1:9–20)

In 1:9, John reports that he received his vision of Christ while on Patmos (a small island in the Aegean Sea where Rome exiled political criminals). Why was John on Patmos? In light of this, how can John relate to his readers (see v. 9)?

- Account of gods word & testimony of Jesus.
- Suffering, temptation, loudiness

John sees an amazing vision of "one like a son of man" (a title that comes from Daniel 7, in which a figure called the son of man receives universal dominion from God himself). Read the descriptions of God, the son of man, and the heavenly messenger in Daniel 7:9–14 and 10:5–6. What are the similarities between these Old Testament passages and the description of Jesus in Revelation 1:12–16? Do you find any surprising similarities? In Revelation 1:12–16, what do you think is the significance of the son of man's snow-white hair? His eyes like a flame of fire? His feet like burnished bronze? His two-edged sword? His face shining like the sun?

In light of how we saw God referred to in 1:4, 8, what is particularly striking about Jesus' self-description in 1:17?

Verse 20 makes clear that "the seven lampstands are the seven churches." So, how might John's vision of the son of man "in the midst of the lampstands" (verse 13) offer comfort to the seven churches of Asia Minor?

2. Seven Letters to Seven Churches (2:1–3:22)

The order of the seven letters to the seven churches (see 1:11) is a clockwise circuit of seven cities, around the route a courier might have taken. But why are *seven* churches singled out rather than six, eight, ten? As we'll see, there are many series of seven in the rest of the book, and seven typically represents fullness and completion. Notice also that each of the seven letters says, "He who has an ear, let him hear what the Spirit says to the *churches* [plural]." What does this tell us about the scope of the intended audience of the letters? In light of this, how should *we* read the letters in Revelation 2–3?

These seven letters are clearly written to encourage suffering churches—but it is a big mistake to think that is their *only* purpose. Look closely at 2:4. What problem does Christ have with the church at Ephesus? If they don't respond to his warning, what will he do (2:5)? What does it mean to "remove your lamp-stand from its place"? In light of this, can you identify another purpose of the letters, in addition to offering comfort?

Having seen that Christ both commends and rebukes the church at Ephesus, read through the other six letters. Which churches receive rebukes? Which ones don't? Which ones are commended? In which matters does Christ find fault with his churches? Which traits or actions please him?

One of the underlying problems for these churches was the enormous cultural pressure to worship the Roman emperor. This was particularly strong in Pergamum, whose Augustus Temple had made it the center of the Roman imperial cult in Asia. In some of the seven churches, certain teachers were urging cultural accommodation. Some Christians were "holding fast" to Christ (2:13), while others were "holding" to the teachings of those who were urging that they just get along with the culture (vv. 14–15). What are some specific ways the church in our day is tempted to accommodate to the broader culture?

Read through the following three sections on *Gospel Glimpses*, *Whole-Bible Connections*, and *Theological Soundings*. Then take time to consider the *Personal Implications* these sections may have for you.

▶ Gospel Glimpses

THE PEOPLE OF GOD. In Revelation 2:9, Jesus says to the church in Smyrna, "I know . . . the slander of those who say that they are Jews and are not, but are a synagogue of Satan." Jesus is speaking of people who actually *are* Jews in an ethnic, religious sense. But in another, deeper sense, they are not Jews (compare Rom. 2:28–29). Being part of God's people is an inward, spiritual reality, not a matter of which family you were born into or an external, religious ceremony or sign. Religious appearances can in fact differ greatly from reality. By opposing the followers of Jesus, the Jews of Smyrna are actually allying themselves with Satan. Jesus doesn't say they are harmless and confused. He says they are a synagogue of Satan (compare John 8:44).

TIME TO REPENT. There's a woman causing serious trouble in the church in Thyatira, influencing some church members to participate in sexual immorality and worship of the pagan gods. Jesus calls her "Jezebel," alluding to the wife of Israel's King Ahab in the Old Testament, who led her husband into worshiping other gods, particularly Baal (1 Kings 16:31; 2 Kings 9:22). Some in the church are being led astray by Jezebel's teaching (Rev. 2:22–23). Jesus' response to Jezebel and her followers is a striking testament to the wideness of his mercy. In 2:21 Jesus says, "I gave her time to repent." In verse 22 he again holds out the possibility of mercy for her followers, saying he will "throw them into great tribulation, *unless they repent of her works.*" Jesus brings judgment on those who refuse to repent, but he gives sinful people every possible opportunity to repent.

▶ Whole-Bible Connections

THE CHURCHES AS LAMPSTANDS. The lampstands in John's vision represent the churches (1:12–13, 20). The word "lampstand" is used in both the Old and New Testaments for the lampstand in the Holy Place of the temple. So, by symbolizing the churches as lampstands, God reminds us of the temple, the place of his presence. The purpose of a local church, like the Old Testament temple before it, is to welcome and house the presence of God (1 Cor. 3:16–17). But there's another important function of a lampstand: it holds a lamp, which gives light. This too is the purpose of local churches, to make God's presence known in the world. In the Sermon on the Mount, Jesus told his disciples, "You are the light of the world. . . . Let your light shine before others, so that they may see your good works and give glory to your Father who is in heaven" (Matt. 5:14, 16). The purpose of a local church in our day is the same as in first-century Asia Minor: to welcome the presence of the living Christ and make his presence known to the world.

THUS SAYS. The phrase "The words of" (in Rev. 2:1, 8, 12, etc.) can be translated, "Thus says." This phrase is sometimes used in the Old Testament to introduce a royal edict (2 Chron. 36:23), and even more often to introduce the words of God himself: "Thus says the LORD . . ." (Amos 1:6, 9, 11). This latter use of the phrase is typical of the prophets and goes all the way back to Moses: "Thus says the LORD, the God of Israel, 'Let my people go'" (Ex. 5:1). It's striking that in Revelation 2:1 and the rest of the seven letters, this phrase is used to introduce the words of the risen Christ. That shouldn't surprise us, because we've already seen John describing Jesus in language used in the Old Testament to describe God himself (i.e., the white hair of the Ancient of Days in Daniel 7). Jesus' words are *God's* words. As such, they are perfect, true, and urgently important.

BALAAM. Jesus charges some in the church in Pergamum with holding to the teaching of Balaam (Rev. 2:14). Numbers 22–24 tells how Balak, the king of Moab, hired the money-loving prophet Balaam (see Deut. 23:4; 2 Pet. 2:15) to curse Israel, but Balaam instead blessed Israel three times (see Deut. 23:5; Josh. 24:9–10; Neh. 13:2; Mic. 6:5). Numbers 25:1–3 reports that even though Midian couldn't defeat Israel *militarily*, they defeated them in another way: Israel began to embrace the gods of Moab, particularly Baal of Peor. We learn in Numbers 31:16 that Balaam taught this strategy to the people of Midian as a means of destroying Israel. In the end, Israel was defeated not through the sword but through friendship and accommodation with other nations and their gods. That is now happening in Pergamum. A group within the church is advocating accommodation to idol feasts, sexual immorality, and worship of the emperor. In every era, God's people must wrestle with how to relate to the culture in which they live. We can't escape culture, nor do we need to. But we must be able to recognize the areas in which Satan is working through our culture, and we must "hold fast" to Christ (2:13) rather than "holding" a policy of ongoing accommodation to Satan and his work (2:14–15).

Theological Soundings

THE NECESSITY OF OBEDIENCE FOR FINAL SALVATION. We see clearly in the seven letters of Revelation 2–3 the necessity of persevering in faith and obedience in order to receive final salvation. For instance, the church in Philadelphia is commanded, "Hold fast what you have, so that no one may seize your crown" (3:11). The "crown" is the crown of life, which represents eternal life. Christians do not *earn* eternal life. It is only the blood of Jesus that frees us from our sins (1:5). But our perseverance in faith and obedience proves that our conversion was genuine and that we were actually Christians to begin with (compare 1 John 2:19).

THE PRESENCE OF THE LAST DAYS. Some interpreters believe Revelation 1:19 provides an outline of the entire book, with chapters 2–3 focusing on the things "that are," and chapters 4–22 focusing on "the things that are to take place after this." Other interpreters, however, are probably right to understand the phrase "after this" as alluding to Daniel 2:28–29, 45, which uses "after this" synonymously with the phrase "the latter days." If this is correct, then at certain key points in the book of Revelation (1:19; 4:1) the phrase "after this" is used to emphasize that the end-time events foreseen by Daniel and the Old Testament prophets have now come to fulfillment through Jesus. In line with the teaching of Jesus (e.g., Luke 11:20) and the rest of the New Testament, the book of Revelation indicates that the first coming of Jesus inaugurated the kingdom of God and the last days. At his second coming, Jesus will bring the consummated kingdom. On this view, both the things "that are" and those that will take place "after this" (1:19) refer to *all* the contents of the book of Revelation.

> ## Personal Implications

Take time to reflect on the implications of Revelation 1:9–3:22 for your own life today. Consider what you have learned that might lead you to praise God, repent of sin, and trust more deeply in his gracious promises. Make notes below on the personal implications for your walk with the Lord of the (1) *Gospel Glimpses*, (2) *Whole-Bible Connections*, (3) *Theological Soundings*, and (4) this passage as a whole.

1. Gospel Glimpses

2. Whole-Bible Connections

3. Theological Soundings

4. Revelation 1:9–3:22

> ## As You Finish This Unit . . .

Take a moment now to ask for the Lord's blessing and help as you continue in this study of Revelation. And take a moment also to look back through this unit of study, to reflect on some key things that the Lord may be teaching you—and perhaps to highlight and underline these things to review again in the future.

Week 4: The Lamb and the Seven Seals

Revelation 4:1–8:1

The Place of the Passage

Now that Jesus has addressed the seven churches, he beckons John into heaven with the promise, "Come up here, and I will show you what must take place after this" (4:1). Before being shown any end-time realities, however, John is granted a magnificent vision of God (Revelation 4) and of the Lamb (Revelation 5). Only then is God's sovereign[1] plan for history (represented by the scroll written within and on the back) revealed, as its seven seals are opened (6:1–8:1).

The Big Picture

Revelation 4:1–8:1 shows us the sovereign authority of God over all things and the supreme worthiness of the Lamb to reveal and implement God's plan.

Reflection and Discussion

Read through the complete passage for this study, Revelation 4:1–8:1. Then review the two passages listed below and write your notes on the following questions concerning John's vision of God and the Lamb (4:1–5:14) and the Lamb's opening of the seals (6:1–8:1). (For further background, see the *ESV Study Bible*, pages 2469–2474, or visit esv.org.)

1. The Lamb Receives the Scroll (4:1–5:14)

John receives an invitation into heaven from "the first voice, which I had heard speaking to me like a trumpet" (4:1). Who is speaking (see 1:10–16)? How does the identity of the speaker heighten the authority of his revelation of "what must take place after this"?

Note that Jesus is doing in 4:1 exactly what God commissioned him to do (see Rev. 1:1). In 1:1 and 4:1, Jesus reveals the things that "must" take place. Why *must* they take place (review the *ESV Study Bible* notes on 1:1 [page 2463])?

After hearing the declaration from the son of man in 4:1, what is John most likely expecting to be shown? What does he see instead in 4:2–11 and 5:1–14 (note that the promise of 4:1 is finally fulfilled in 6:1–7:17)?

How does the vision in 4:1–11 highlight the beauty, character, and power of God?

The scroll introduced in 5:1–4 symbolizes God's sovereign plan (see 4:1) for history. John begins weeping, since no one is worthy to open the scroll and its seven seals (thus disclosing and implementing God's plan). But John is then told that the Lion of the tribe of Judah has conquered, so that "he can open the scroll and its seven seals" (5:5). What is surprising about what John sees immediately following, in 5:6? What does this vision tell us about how Jesus "conquered"?

How does John's vision of the Lamb in 5:6–14 highlight the Lamb's salvific achievement and his deity?

Why do you think John is shown the sovereign authority of God (4:1–11) and the Lamb (5:1–14) *before* being shown the plan God has ordained and the Lamb will implement (6:1–8:1)?

2. The Lamb Opens the Seven Seals (6:1–8:1)

The views of interpreters of Revelation diverge considerably concerning the opening of the seven seals. Many "futurists" (who understand the events of Revelation 4–22 to refer to events still future to twenty-first-century readers) believe that the opening of the first seal begins the great tribulation. Many "idealists" (who believe the events of Revelation 4–22 range over the entire span of time between the first and second comings of Christ) believe that some of the seals refer to ongoing realities in the inter-advent age. The first four seals clearly form a group, since they bring forth four horses and horsemen. What do these horses and their riders represent?

The fifth seal shows the souls of believers killed for their faithful witness to Jesus. What is their question, and how is it answered in the verses that follow 6:9–11 (see verses 16–17)?

The sixth seal shows the enemies of God at the final judgment, the destruction of the first heaven and earth. How is the awesome severity of God's judgment displayed? What question is asked by God's enemies? How is it answered (see 7:9)?

In 7:1–17, we encounter an interlude before the opening of the seventh seal in 8:1. Again, futurist and idealist interpretations diverge. Many futurists understand the 144,000 to be a literal number of ethnic Jews who come to faith during the great tribulation, after the church has been raptured to heaven. On this view, the 144,000 in 7:1–8 are a different group from the great multitude in 7:9–17. However, many idealists understand the 144,000 Jews in 7:1–8 to be a symbolic representation of God's new covenant people, so that it is the *same* group as the great multitude in 7:9–17. In either case, how is God's provision and protection of his people emphasized in these verses?

The seventh seal in 8:1 reveals silence in heaven for half an hour. What is the significance of this abrupt and shocking silence?

Read through the following three sections on *Gospel Glimpses, Whole-Bible Connections,* and *Theological Soundings.* Then take time to consider the *Personal Implications* these sections may have for you.

Gospel Glimpses

CONQUERING THROUGH "DEFEAT." The Lion of the tribe of Judah, the Root of David, has "conquered." But how? We see in 5:6 that he conquered by being slain as a Lamb. It was an ironic victory—victory through apparent defeat. We're told by the 24 elders that it was precisely Jesus' death that makes him "worthy" to implement God's sovereign plan for the world (5:9–10). Jesus is the conquering Lion *because* he's the conquered Lamb! Now, risen, he has seven horns and seven eyes (5:6)—horns represent power, so seven horns represent complete power. The seven eyes are the seven spirits, representing the Holy Spirit's activity throughout the earth. The Lamb who was slain now has all

31

power and sees everything. Jesus' ironic victory sets the pattern for his followers, who "conquer" through their faithful suffering. This is the gospel way.

▶ Whole-Bible Connections

GOD'S SEAL. Revelation 7:3 says the "servants of our God" are to be sealed on their foreheads. God's seal indicates ownership (compare Rev. 14:1). In the ancient world, it was common practice for a master to mark his slaves on their foreheads as proof of ownership (notice it is the "servants" of God whom God seals). God's seal also indicates his protection, as is made clear from the background in Ezekiel 9, where God spares his people from execution by placing a mark on their foreheads. This in turn recalls the Passover, when the angel of death passed over every house of Israel that had the blood of the Passover lamb on its lintel, but killed every firstborn of the Egyptians (Exodus 12). The seal of Revelation 7 makes clear that God continues to protect his people.

OLD TESTAMENT EXPECTATION, NEW TESTAMENT FULFILLMENT. There is a parallel between Revelation 5:5–6 and Revelation 7:1–17. In Revelation 5, John *hears* about the Lion of the tribe of Judah (an Old Testament picture of the Messiah). He then *sees* a Lamb (Jesus, the New Testament fulfillment). The New Testament fulfillment is unexpected and surprising: the Lion has conquered by being slain, as a lamb. What we see with the 144,000 in Revelation 7 is closely parallel to this. In 7:4, John *hears* an Old Testament expectation: "the number of the sealed, 144,000, sealed from every tribe of the sons of Israel." In 7:9, John *sees* an unexpected New Testament fulfillment of this expectation: not just ethnic Jews, but rather "a great multitude that no one could number, from every nation, from all tribes and peoples and languages, standing before the throne and before the Lamb." This indicates that the 144,000 in 7:4–8 is the *same group* as the great multitude in 7:9–17, but pictured in two different ways (Old Testament expectation and New Testament fulfillment), just as the Lion and the Lamb in Revelation 5:5–6 both represent *Jesus*, pictured in two different ways (Old Testament expectation and New Testament fulfillment).

THE SOUND OF SILENCE. The silence in heaven at the opening of the seventh seal is sudden and shocking. Throughout Revelation 1–7, we have heard a joyous cacophony of sound reverberating throughout heaven (e.g., 1:10; 4:5, 8, 11; 5:9–10, 12–13). But now, suddenly, silence for half an hour. What's the meaning of this unexpected silence? The Old Testament background helps us understand. In the book of Zephaniah, God announces his coming terrible, worldwide judgment (Zeph. 1:2). Zephaniah 1:7 tells us the proper response: "Be silent before the Lord GOD! For the day of the LORD is near." In the Old Testament—and in Revelation—silence is the horrified, awe-filled, stunned response to the sheer weight of God's judgment (see Hab. 2:20).

Theological Soundings

THE DEITY OF CHRIST. If we compare the worship of the angels in 5:12 to the worship of the 24 elders in 4:11, we see something astonishing. Three of the exact same words (glory, honor, power) are repeated in 5:12, but now they're ascribed not to God the Father, but to the Lamb. It's clear that in Revelation 5 Jesus shares in the worship due only to the one true God: "And I heard every creature in heaven and on earth and under the earth and in the sea, and all that is in them, saying, 'To him who sits on the throne *and to the Lamb* be blessing and honor and glory and might forever and ever!' And the four living creatures said, 'Amen!' and the elders fell down *and worshiped*" (vv. 13–14). Jesus is worshiped as divine because he is God.

THE ATONING SIGNIFICANCE OF JESUS' DEATH. As noted in "Gospel Glimpses" above, Jesus' ironic victory at the cross is a model for the "overcoming" of suffering Christians. But while Jesus' death serves as a model for suffering believers, it is also unique in its effect. It achieves what the death of believers cannot achieve. The faithful believer named Antipas, though killed for his faith (2:13), did not redeem anyone through his death. Why is Jesus' death uniquely redemptive? Part of the explanation is that Jesus is divine. He dies not for his own sin (as God, he is perfect) but for the sins of others. Moreover, because he is God, he is uniquely able to bear the infinite weight of the Father's punishment. Therefore, his death achieves a great victory by ransoming people for God.

Personal Implications

Take time to reflect on the implications of Revelation 4:1–8:1 for your own life today. Consider what you have learned that might lead you to praise God, repent of sin, and trust more deeply in his gracious promises. Make notes below on the personal implications for your walk with the Lord of the (1) *Gospel Glimpses*, (2) *Whole-Bible Connections*, (3) *Theological Soundings*, and (4) this passage as a whole.

1. Gospel Glimpses

2. Whole-Bible Connections

3. Theological Soundings

4. Revelation 4:1–8:1

> ### As You Finish This Unit . . .

Take a moment now to ask for the Lord's blessing and help as you continue in this study of Revelation. And take a moment also to look back through this unit of study, to reflect on some key things that the Lord may be teaching you—and perhaps to highlight and underline these things to review again in the future.

Definitions

[1] **Sovereignty** – Supreme and independent power and authority. Sovereignty over all things is a distinctive attribute of God (1 Tim. 6:15–16). He directs all things to carry out his purposes (Rom. 8:28–29).

WEEK 5: THE SEVEN ANGELS AND SEVEN TRUMPETS

Revelation 8:2–11:19

The Place of the Passage

By the time we arrive at Revelation 8:2, we have seen a vast sweep of redemptive history, including the first coming of Jesus (1:5); the struggles of first-century Christians and churches (chs. 2–3); the present age between Jesus' first and second comings (6:1–8); the final judgment (6:12–17); and the new creation (7:9–17). Now, in 8:2–11:19, John's vision of the seven trumpets covers that same time period again, this time giving additional theological insight into God's purposes and his terrible judgments.

The Big Picture

John's vision of the seven trumpets communicates the severity of God's judgment—and also the greatness of his mercy—toward those who unrepentantly oppose him.

> **Reflection and Discussion**

Read through the complete passage for this study, Revelation 8:2–11:19. Then review the two passages listed below and write your notes on the following questions. (For further background, see the *ESV Study Bible*, pages 2474–2479, or visit esv.org.)

1. Prayers Go Up; Fire Comes Down (8:2–5)

In these verses, the prayers of the saints ascend to God with incense from the golden censer (vv. 3–4). In light of 6:9–11, what do you think is the focus of the saints' prayers in 8:3–4?

The saints' prayers go up to God with the incense of the censer—then that same censer is filled with fire from the altar and flung down upon the earth. Clearly, the throwing of the censer is an *answer* to the prayers of the saints. What do you think is symbolized by the flinging of the fire-filled censer from heaven to earth? (Note the thunder, lightning, and earthquake mentioned in 8:5.)

Importantly, all the divine judgments of 8:6–11:19 are God's response to the prayers of his people.

2. The Seven Trumpets Are Blown (8:6–11:19)

Futurist interpreters of Revelation understand the seven trumpets to refer to yet-future judgments from God that will come upon his enemies in the great tribulation, after the church has been raptured. It seems on balance more likely, however, that the first six trumpets actually cover the entire period of the present age, from the first coming of Jesus to his second coming, just as the seven seals did (the idealist position). But what about the seventh trumpet? Recall that the sixth and seventh seals described the final judgment. Now read the description of the seventh trumpet in 11:15–19. What time period do you think these verses most likely describe?

Interpreters differ on exactly what the first four trumpets represent, and how literally (or figuratively) to interpret them. But even more important than these details is the theological significance of the trumpets. How does 8:2 emphasize God's direct hand in the trumpet judgments (see also v. 7)?

Consider the nature and purpose of a trumpet. Read Ezekiel 33:3–4. How does the blowing of seven *trumpets* highlight God's mercy? Notice also the repeated indication of what part of the earth, sea, and heavens are destroyed or darkened. In what way does this divine mercy increase the tragedy of 9:20–21?

How does the eagle's cry in 8:13 indicate an escalation in the severity of judgments from the first four trumpets to the last three? The first four trumpets brought judgment upon the earth, waters, and sky; where does judgment fall in the last three trumpets? Satan and his demons[1] are the ones who bring the judgment, but how is God's sovereign control emphasized (see 9:1, 3–5, 14)?

Just as we saw an interlude in Revelation 7:1–17 before the opening of the seventh seal, so now we have an interlude in Revelation 10:1–11:14 before the blowing of the seventh trumpet. First, in 10:1–11, we see a magnificent angel handing John a "little scroll" that is sweet in his mouth but bitter in his stomach. How does this interaction between the angel and John underscore John's authority?

The second part of the interlude is Revelation 11:1–14, which includes instructions for John to measure "the temple of God and the altar and those who worship there" (vv. 1–2) as well as a vision of the two prophets who are killed and then raised to life (vv. 3–14). Like the two visions between the sixth and seventh seals (the 144,000 and the international multitude), these two visions of the temple and the two witnesses between the sixth and seventh trumpets likely symbolize a single reality: God's protection of his suffering people. How are God's provision and protection emphasized?

Read through the following three sections on *Gospel Glimpses, Whole-Bible Connections,* and *Theological Soundings*. Then take time to consider the *Personal Implications* these sections may have for you.

Gospel Glimpses

THE MERCY IN THE TRUMPETS. As every parent or sibling of a young, aspiring trumpet player knows, trumpets are *loud*. In the Old Testament, trumpets were used to warn of coming judgment (Ezek. 33:3–4). That's their purpose also in Revelation 8–11, even though the warning is rejected (9:20–21). Even God's judgments are meant to warn sinners from their sin. And note that God's judgment through the trumpets is not complete judgment—it destroys one-third of things on earth, sea, and sky, not everything. Even in judgment, God remembers mercy.

THE FULLNESS OF GOD'S JUDGMENT AND MERCY. Sometimes what is *not* said is as important as what is said. When we compare the descriptions of God in 1:4, 8 and 4:8 with the description in 11:17, the omission of "and who is to come" is striking. Why is it not included in 11:17? Because in this vision of the final future, God has *already* come. That's the point of the song of the 24 elders, who thank God for having come to judge his enemies and reward his people. In 11:15–19, we're granted a glorious gospel vision of God's fulfillment of all his promises.

Whole-Bible Connections

RECAPITULATION IN THE PROPHETS AND REVELATION. Futurist interpreters see a chronological sequence between the seven seals in Revelation 6–8, the seven trumpets in Revelation 8–11, and the seven bowls in Revelation 16. However, it seems more likely that, rather than being ordered as a straight chronology, the book of Revelation is organized in a number of sections that cover the same chronological ground over and over again. This way of organizing a book is called "recapitulation." Tellingly, we find recapitulation in the Old Testament prophetic books that most influenced the writing of Revelation. For instance, in Daniel 2 and 7, the same sequence of events is described using different symbols. Similarly, in Revelation, the seals, the trumpets, and the bowls describe events that occur during this present age, between the first and second comings of Jesus. Why go over the same chronological ground multiple times? The four gospel accounts of Jesus' life point toward an answer: each of the gospels (and each of John's visions) offers additional theological insight into the same events.

THE PLAGUES. The seven trumpet judgments recall the 10 plagues God brought upon Egypt immediately before Israel's exodus.[2] For instance, the first trumpet (hail and fire) recalls the seventh Egyptian plague; the second and third trumpets (the sea turning to blood, water sources being ruined) recalls the first plague; and the fourth trumpet (the heavenly bodies darkened) recalls the ninth plague. In fact, the word "plague" is used in Revelation 9:18, 20, and the related verb is used in 8:12. This background of the Egyptian plagues is important, because it shows that the trumpet blasts bring judgment from God upon those who reject him, just as the Egyptian plagues brought divine judgment upon the false gods and the recalcitrant ruler of Egypt. God spared the Israelites and judged his enemies.

GOD'S KINGDOM. One of the central motifs of the Bible is the kingdom of God. In the Old Testament period, God's people understood that he was the great King of the whole world (Ps. 29:10). But they longed for the day when God would fully assert his reign by judging his enemies and vindicating his people (Isa. 24:21–23). They understood that the great day of the Lord would usher in this kingdom (Isa. 13:6–7; 28:5). Jesus' radical and surprising teaching about the kingdom of God was that it had come in an inaugurated form through his ministry (Luke 11:20–22). It came in a hidden manner, like a seed (Luke 13:18–19), not in the expected public, spectacular fashion. However, Jesus also taught that the kingdom would eventually come in all its glorious splendor (Matt. 13:43). We see the ultimate fulfillment of this teaching in Revelation 11:15–19: "The kingdom of the world has become the kingdom of our Lord and of his Christ, and he shall reign forever and ever" (v. 15).

▶ Theological Soundings

SATAN AND HIS DEMONS. In the twenty-first-century Western world, the existence of Satan and his demons is often dismissed out of hand. They don't fit within an anti-supernaturalistic worldview. But the fifth trumpet, in 9:1–12, is most likely a description of both Satan (vv. 1–2, 11) and his demons (vv. 3–10). If that is the case, we learn several important things about them. They are a powerful force, to be taken seriously. They can severely torment unbelievers (vv. 4–6). However, they are always under the sovereign authority of God—note that Satan "was given the key to the shaft of the bottomless pit" (v. 1) and that demons "were allowed to torment" people for a limited period of time (v. 5). Neither demons nor Satan are an equal-and-opposite power to God. They, like all the created universe, are under the sovereign hand of the Creator.

SOME THINGS WE DO NOT KNOW. In Revelation, there are seven seals, seven trumpets, and seven bowls. There are also seven thunders, though most people don't know about them. There's a reason for that: "When [the angel] called out, the seven thunders sounded. And when the seven thunders had sounded, I was about to write, but I heard a voice from heaven saying, 'Seal up what the seven thunders have said, and do not write it down'" (10:3–4). John is to keep the message of the seven thunders secret by not writing what they reveal. This is an important reminder for all readers of Revelation. God reveals some things to us, but not all things. We know only the "outskirts of his ways" (Job 26:14). Realizing this should humble us before his sovereign wisdom, but also strengthen us in hope, as we realize that God has purposes and plans we do not know, for events and circumstances we do not understand.

▶ Personal Implications

Take time to reflect on the implications of Revelation 8:2–11:19 for your own life today. Consider what you have learned that might lead you to praise God, repent of sin, and trust more deeply in his gracious promises. Make notes below on the personal implications for your walk with the Lord of the (1) *Gospel Glimpses*, (2) *Whole-Bible Connections*, (3) *Theological Soundings*, and (4) this passage as a whole.

1. Gospel Glimpses

2. Whole-Bible Connections

3. Theological Soundings

4. Revelation 8:2–11:19

As You Finish This Unit . . .

Take a moment now to ask for the Lord's blessing and help as you continue in this study of Revelation. And take a moment also to look back through this unit of study, to reflect on some key things that the Lord may be teaching you—and perhaps to highlight and underline these things to review again in the future.

Definitions

[1] **Demon** – an evil spirit that can inhabit a human being and influence him or her to carry out its will. Demons are fallen angels who were created by God and are always limited by God. Jesus and his followers cast out many demons, demonstrating Jesus' superiority over them. All demons will one day be destroyed along with Satan (Matt. 25:41; Rev. 20:10).

[2] **Exodus** – the departure of the people of Israel from Egypt and their journey to Mount Sinai under Moses' leadership (Exodus 1–19; Numbers 33). The exodus demonstrated God's power and providence for his people, who had been enslaved by the Egyptians. The annual festival of Passover commemorates God's final plague upon the Egyptians, resulting in Israel's release from Egypt.

WEEK 6: THE COSMIC CONFLICT BETWEEN CHRIST AND SATAN

Revelation 12:1–14:20

The Place of the Passage

Revelation 12 is the pivot point of the book of Revelation. Chapters 1–11 have shown us the conflict the churches face within (e.g., false teachers) and without (e.g., the Roman empire). Now we get a clear view of the spiritual reality behind and beneath that conflict. Chapters 12–14 identify the main enemies of Christians: the devil, the beast from the sea, the beast from the earth, and Babylon. Then, in chapters 15–22, we see those enemies *destroyed*, in reverse order: Babylon, the beasts, and finally Satan himself.[1] The dominoes are set up and then toppled.

The Big Picture

This pivotal section of Revelation shows the satanic opposition Christians face but also reminds readers that, through the work of Jesus, Satan has already been defeated.

Reflection and Discussion

Read through the complete passage for this study, Revelation 12:1–14:20. Then write your notes on the following questions. (For further background, see the *ESV Study Bible*, pages 2479–2484, or visit esv.org.)

There are three main characters in the opening vision of 12:1–6: a woman in labor, a male child, and a great red dragon. Compare 12:1 with Joseph's dream in Genesis 37:9. Whom do you think the woman symbolizes? Compare the description of the male child with the description of God's Messiah in Psalm 2:9. Who is the male child? Compare Revelation 12:3 and 12:9. Who is the great red dragon?

In 12:1–6, we see there is a conflict deeper than the one between God's people (the woman) and Satan (the dragon), namely, the conflict between Satan and Christ. Satan seeks to destroy Jesus (compare Matt. 2:16–18). According to Revelation 12:5, what is the outcome of this conflict? Who wins?

Revelation 12:5 gives a broad-brush overview of Jesus' victory over Satan, moving immediately from his birth to his resurrection and ascension to God's heavenly throne. In 12:7–12, we're granted another perspective on the conflict between Jesus and Satan, with more details filled in. The loud voice in verse 10 announces God's victory and Satan's defeat. Noting that Satan is described as "the accuser of our brothers . . . , who accuses them day and night before our

God," how do Jesus' death, resurrection, and ascension defeat Satan's accusations of believers before God?

Revelation 12:11 describes Christians who "conquer" the devil even though he kills them (compare the same word "conquer" in 13:7)! In what sense do believers conquer Satan? Do they look to the world like conquerors?

How might 12:12 encourage Christians suffering the fierce attacks of Satan? Does the dragon's anger show that he is winning . . . or losing? How does 12:13–17 emphasize God's protection and care for his people?

In Revelation 13, we meet two agents of Satan's plans: the beast from the sea (13:1–10) and the beast from the land (13:11–18), also known as the false prophet (compare 16:13; 19:20; 20:10). The beast from the sea may point ultimately toward an end-time individual (the Antichrist in 1 John 2:18, or the "man of lawlessness" in 2 Thess. 2:3–4). But there are also surely partial fulfillments represented by anti-Christian governments throughout this age (note the multiple kingdoms represented by the four beasts from the sea in Daniel 7—beasts that are remarkably similar to the beast in Rev. 13:1–2). Even more immediately, in John's day the beast symbolizes the Roman empire, and its recovery from a "mortal wound" symbolizes the wildly fluctuating fortunes of Rome in the period after Nero's death. The second beast, the "false prophet," refers to the cult of the worship of the Roman emperor, since the false prophet is said to make "the earth and its inhabitants worship the first beast" (13:12). But again, this beast also finds partial fulfillment in the false religions, philosophies, and ideologies that arise throughout this present age.

In 14:1–5, we meet the 144,000 for the second time (compare 7:1–8). As with their first appearance, the 144,000 most likely represent *all* God's people, not just Jewish believers who have trusted in Jesus during the great tribulation. They are depicted as God's holy army (7:3–8; 14:1–5)—an army that conquers, ironically, by being faithful unto death. How does Revelation 14:6–20 emphasize God's sovereign provision for his people? To what does it call God's people? (See 14:12; compare 13:10.)

Read through the following three sections on *Gospel Glimpses*, *Whole-Bible Connections*, and *Theological Soundings*. Then take time to consider the *Personal Implications* these sections may have for you.

▶ Gospel Glimpses

NO ACCUSATION WILL STAND. Before the cross and resurrection of Jesus, Satan could accuse God's people by arguing that their sin hadn't been atoned for, since the blood of bulls and goats wasn't sufficient for the task and God had simply "passed over" the sins of his people, that is, taken no action of any kind with regard to them (see Rom. 3:25). But through Jesus' death, God made full atonement for the sins of his people. After the cross, Satan's grounds for accusation are demonstrably invalid. He accuses in vain. This is why the voice from heaven says, "the accuser of our brothers has been thrown down" (Rev. 12:10). Satan's power has been decisively broken.

AN ETERNAL GOSPEL. The "gospel," which in Greek means "good news," is the declaration that God through Christ extends a gracious offer of righteousness to those who will receive it. However, Revelation 14:6–13 helps us understand another aspect of the gospel. John sees an angel flying overhead, "with an eternal gospel to proclaim to those who dwell on earth" (v. 6). The following verses call people to fear God in light of his judgment (v. 7), which is graphically described in verses 8–11. We learn in this passage that while the gospel is truly the good news of God's wonderful mercy, it also has a "judicial" side—the message of God's perfect, totally righteous justice, displayed in full retribution for our sins, visited upon Jesus in our place on the cross.

Whole-Bible Connections

THE 1,260 DAYS. Revelation 12:6 says the woman (God's people) was nourished in the wilderness for 1,260 days, or (in v. 14) "for a time, and times, and half a time" (if "a time" equals one year, that's 3-1/2 years, equivalent to 1,260 days). We've already seen in Revelation 11:2 that the temple is trampled for 42 months (again, equivalent to 1,260 days), and that the two witnesses in Revelation 11:3 prophesy for 1,260 days. Why all these references to 3-1/2 years = 42 months = 1,260 days? As with most symbols in Revelation, the answer is found in the Old Testament background. The phrase "a time, times, and half a time" comes from Daniel 7:25 and 12:7, where it refers to a period of tribulation for God's people. In Revelation, this tribulation is understood to have begun already with the first coming of Jesus, lasting until his return. The wilderness of this world (Rev. 12:6) therefore has a dual character. It is a time of tribulation and testing, but also of divine provision. The woman in Revelation 12 "flees" to the wilderness because she is in danger. But she goes to a place "prepared by God, in which she is to be nourished."

GOD'S SON, THE MESSIAH. Psalm 2 is one of the great messianic psalms in the Psalter. It speaks of God choosing David and his descendants as the royal house of Israel, and it calls the nations to receive the blessing God originally promised them through Israel (see Gen. 12:1–3) by submitting to David and his heirs. All nations who reject the rule of God and his anointed King (Ps. 2:1–3) will incur the wrath of God (vv. 4–6) instead of the blessing that God would pour out on them through their submission (vv. 10–12). Psalm 2 is interpreted as a reference to Jesus in the New Testament (see Heb. 1:5), and it also stands behind Revelation 11:18 and 12:5. The message of the allusions is that Jesus is the true King who brings God's judgment and blessing to the world.

Theological Soundings

SATANIC IMITATION. In Revelation 12:9, Satan is called "the deceiver of the whole world." He attempts to destroy God's people by pouring water "like a river out of his mouth" (12:15), probably a reference to his deceptive words. So, it is not surprising that Satan attempts to deceive the world by imitating God. Note the following striking parallels between God and Satan (see the *ESV Study Bible*, page 2481): (1) God exists as a Trinity: Father, Son, and Spirit; there is also a false satanic trinity comprised of the dragon, the beast from the sea, and the beast from the land. (2) The Lamb was killed and then raised to life; in parallel, the beast from the sea recovers from a mortal wound. (3) God seals his saints, writing his name on their foreheads (14:1); the beast from the land requires his servants to receive his mark on their right hand or forehead (13:16). (4) The church is represented as a bride clothed in white; and the world kingdoms (in particular, the city of Rome) are represented as a prostitute clothed in purple and scarlet. Satan operates through imitative deception; he disguises himself as an angel of light, and Jesus' followers should expect similar tactics from Satan's servants (2 Cor. 11:14–15).

HELL. Revelation 14:11 provides a sobering picture of God's eternal judgment of his enemies: "And the smoke of their torment goes up forever and ever, and they have no rest, day or night, these worshipers of the beast and its image, and whoever receives the mark of its name." This description indicates two things. First, hell lasts forever for the human enemies of God, just as it does for the devil (compare Rev. 20:10). Second, those who exist in hell are not annihilated, but rather experience eternal, conscious suffering (the word for "torment" is always used in Revelation to indicate conscious suffering, never annihilation).

▶ Personal Implications

Take time to reflect on the implications of Revelation 12:1–14:20 for your own life today. Consider what you have learned that might lead you to praise God, repent of sin, and trust more deeply in his gracious promises. Make notes below on the personal implications for your walk with the Lord of the (1) *Gospel Glimpses*, (2) *Whole-Bible Connections*, (3) *Theological Soundings*, and (4) this passage as a whole.

1. Gospel Glimpses

2. Whole-Bible Connections

3. Theological Soundings

4. Revelation 12:1–14:20

> ## As You Finish This Unit . . .

Take a moment now to ask for the Lord's blessing and help as you continue in this study of Revelation. And take a moment also to look back through this unit of study, to reflect on some key things that the Lord may be teaching you—and perhaps to highlight and underline these things to review again in the future.

Definitions

[1] **Satan** – a spiritual being whose name means "accuser." As the leader of all the demonic forces, he opposes God's rule and seeks to harm God's people and accuse them of wrongdoing. His power, however, is confined to the bounds that God has set for him, and one day he will be destroyed along with all his demons (Matt. 25:41; Rev. 20:10).

WEEK 7: THE SEVEN ANGELS AND SEVEN BOWLS

Revelation 15:1–16:21

▲

The Place of the Passage

We encountered seven seals, seven thunders, and seven trumpets in Revelation 6–11. Chapters 12–14 then focused on the key enemies of God (particularly Satan and the two beasts) before providing yet another view of God's final victory over his enemies (as we've seen, the end of history and the final judgment is depicted numerous times throughout the book, e.g., 6:12–17; 11:17–19; 14:14–20). Now, in Revelation 15–16, we're presented with the last major cycle of seven: the seven bowls.

The Big Picture

This passage depicts the climactic outpouring of the judgments of God (ch. 16) after first affirming the righteousness and justice of the God who inflicts such terrible retribution (ch. 15).

> ## Reflection and Discussion

Read through the complete passage for this study, Revelation 15:1–16:21. Then review the shorter passages below and write your own notes on the following questions. (For further background, see the *ESV Study Bible*, pages 2484–2486, or visit esv.org.)

1. Heaven's Sanctuary Is Filled with Glory (15:1–8)

Notice that verse 1 introduces the "seven plagues" by emphasizing their climactic nature. Futurist interpreters of Revelation understand the seven plagues/bowls as referring to God's judgments at the end of history, before Christ's establishment of the millennial kingdom. At least some idealist interpreters, on the other hand, understand the plagues/bowls as covering the same chronological period as the seals and trumpets: namely, the present age between the first and second comings of Jesus. According to this view, John's statement that the plagues are "the last" (v. 1) indicates that they are the last of the sevenfold visions in the book of Revelation (not that they are chronologically last in history). They therefore represent God's climactic judgments throughout this age, which are reserved for those of God's enemies who refuse to repent.

After verse 1, we are prepared to encounter the terrible judgments of a wrath-filled God. But scan down through the passage: where, surprisingly, do we actually see the enactment of the plagues/bowls announced in 15:1? What are some possible reasons why verses 2–8 come where they do, between the announcement and the enactment of the plagues?

No.
Tough The reason things come as a break
is to explain how ~~meana~~ this wrath is
Good and just.

In 15:2–4, we overhear God's people singing a song with two titles: the "song of Moses" and the "song of the Lamb." Why are there two titles? Why these particular titles, since neither Moses nor the Lamb appears in the song? What does the song teach us about God? Why are these attributes of God so important for us to hear and believe before encountering the bowl judgments in Revelation 16? *Similar themes.*

Song of Moses (Great deeds, Just and true, all nations come to worship)
God is just, true, holy.
Need to remember these characteristics before the wrath comes (maybe to just those who reject God).

Notice that the song emphasizes God's justice and truth, his holiness and his righteous acts. The judgments about to fall are particularly terrible, so it is crucial to be reminded that they come from a perfectly holy God. Moreover, notice that God's kingship over the nations is emphasized. God's sovereignty extends throughout the earth. We will see that God's judgment through the bowls is comprehensive in a manner not true of the seals or the trumpets (compare, e.g., 6:8; 8:9; and 16:3).

In this "final" 7 bowls of wrath there are no partial measures.

Again, given the severity of the coming judgments, why is it important for us to see, in 15:5–8, where the plagues originate from? Notice the attention given to the "sanctuary of the tent of witness" (a very holy place) and the description of the seven angels "clothed in pure, bright linen." What does this tell us about nature of the bowl judgments?

They are intentional actions on God's part. They come from Him and are not outside of his control.

2. The Seven Bowls Are Poured Out (16:1–21)

The first four trumpet judgments in 8:7–12 affect the earth, sea, fresh water sources, and the heavens. Note that the first four bowls in 16:2–9 affect the same spheres. However, what is the difference between the trumpets and the bowls in terms of the *extent* of the judgments? Note also that, unlike the seal and trumpet judgments, there is no pause or interlude between the sixth and seventh bowls. All these observations point toward the climactic nature of these judgments.

In what ways do the words of the angel (16:5–6) and the altar (16:7) confirm the theme of the "song of the Lamb" in 15:3–4?

They are the same and importan reminders right in the middle of the plauges.

· God is just and true.

Note that those being judged by God refuse to repent (16:9–11, 21). How does this emphasize the justice of God's judgments?

He previously offered forgiveness and there is harsh judment against those who don't repent

The sixth bowl dries up the river Euphrates (16:12), making way for the "kings from the east" (perhaps the Parthians, on Rome's eastern border) to wage war. But Satan and his henchmen plan to stir up a much bigger war. Note that demonic spirits come out of the *mouths* of the dragon, the beast, and the prophet (16:13), emphasizing their deceptive influence on the nations. The kings of the whole world are duped into believing they can conquer God and his Messiah (16:14, 16).

Why do you think Jesus cuts into the vision of the sixth bowl with his urgent word in verse 15?

as a reminder that he will appear unexpectedly and with power.

Compare the seventh bowl in 16:17–21 with what we've already seen in Revelation, in the sixth seal (6:12–17); the vision of final destruction in 11:13; and the seventh trumpet (11:19). Now compare with 20:11 and 21:1. What are the similarities? The differences? The seventh bowl is clearly a climactic picture of God's final judgment upon the sinful world.

7th bowl = "It is done", lightning, thunder, earthquake
6th seal = Sun black, moon blood, earthquakes
Vision 11:13 = a Great earth quake, 7000 dead!

Similarity = earthquakes & something happening to the sky.
Differences = "It's done" vs partial destruction

Read through the following three sections on *Gospel Glimpses, Whole-Bible Connections*, and *Theological Soundings*. Then take time to consider the *Personal Implications* these sections may have for you.

Gospel Glimpses

A BEAUTIFUL INTERRUPTION. Jesus interrupts the description of the sixth bowl with a call to receive divine blessing: "Blessed is the one who stays awake, keeping his garments on, that he may not go about naked and be seen exposed!" (16:15). This is the third of seven benedictions[1] scattered throughout Revelation (see the *ESV Study Bible*, page 2484). It's a beautiful reminder that, even amid the chaos of demonic activity and the raging of the nations, God can bless his people. Jesus *wants* this blessing for his followers. That's why he cuts right into the vision to urge them to stay awake, dressed for action.

A SPEAKING ALTAR. In Revelation, strange things happen. In 16:7, the altar speaks: "Yes, Lord God the Almighty, true and just are your judgments!" We see God's merciful care for his people when we recall that the heavenly altar is the very place where the souls of the martyrs are gathered, crying out to God for justice (6:9–10). This connection demonstrates that God has remembered the suffering of his people.

Whole-Bible Connections

A SONG WITH TWO TITLES. The song sung by the conquerors is called "the song of Moses, the servant of God" and "the song of the Lamb." We're reminded of Exodus 15:1–18, where "Moses and the people of Israel sang [a] song to the LORD" after God drowned the Egyptian army in the Red Sea. That song was a magnificent celebration of God's power, which smashed the world's most impressive army. Now, those who have remained "faithful unto death" (Rev. 2:10) stand beside the sea of glass (15:2; a reference to the transparent pavement surrounding God's throne) and sing a song of God's victory through the Lamb, Jesus Christ. This song draws heavily on Old Testament language, and is the only song in Revelation to use the typical parallelism of Hebrew poetry. We're meant to see that the God of the Old Testament is the same God victorious now in Christ. However, his redemptive work through Christ is far greater than anything that has gone before.

ARMAGEDDON. In 16:14, 16, the kings of the earth assemble at Armageddon "for battle on the great day of God the Almighty." Throughout the Old Testament, the plain of Megiddo (about a two-day walk north of Jerusalem) was a site of important battles. In Judges 5:19–21, God is praised for having defeated there an overwhelmingly powerful force of the enemies of his people. This divine victory in Judges 5 is a type of the great, final victory that God wins for his people at Armageddon (compare Rev. 16:16; 19:17–21; 20:7–10).

▶ Theological Soundings

GOD'S HOLINESS AND HIS JUDGMENT. Some theologians pit God's holiness[2] against his judgment, as though excuses or apologies must be made for God's wrath-filled judgments, or as though the wrath-filled God of the Old Testament is pleasantly softened into a more merciful version in the New Testament. But Revelation 15–16 shows how badly mistaken are these views. God's judgments in these chapters are more severe than those in the Old Testament. In Revelation, God's judgments do not undermine his holiness. Rather, they *demonstrate* it. Note that the seven bowl judgments issue from God's holy tent (15:5), the place of his glory (15:8). The description in 15:8 alludes to the consecrations of the tabernacle (Ex. 40:34–35) and the temple (1 Kings 8:10–11). God's glory, his holy character, is demonstrated through (not obscured by) his righteous judgments on his sinful enemies.

THE HARDENING OF GOD'S ENEMIES. In Revelation 16:21, we see that God's climactic judgment does not lead to repentance. Rather, those under it continue to rebel, cursing God: "And great hailstones, about one hundred pounds each, fell from heaven on people; and they cursed God for the plague of the hail, because the plague was so severe." C. S. Lewis once wrote that the gates of hell are locked on the inside. In the end, God's enemies are hardened in their sin, not sorry for it. Their rebellion continues forever.

> ### Personal Implications

Take time to reflect on the implications of Revelation 15:1–16:21 for your own life today. Consider what you have learned that might lead you to praise God, repent of sin, and trust more deeply in his gracious promises. Make notes below on the personal implications for your walk with the Lord of the (1) *Gospel Glimpses*, (2) *Whole-Bible Connections*, (3) *Theological Soundings*, and (4) this passage as a whole.

1. Gospel Glimpses

God comes in the midst of Chaos and sin. This made me also think about how he comes also in the mundane or quiet as well.

2. Whole-Bible Connections

God defeats the enemies of Him and His people. In smaller examples through history but also final ones too. There will be a final battle and we already know who wins. Brings balance to the smaller battles lost along the way.

3. Theological Soundings

He is the same God (then & now & forever) Sometimes punishment does not lead to repentance, and the holy spirit is needed for that. We can't socially engineer the perfect follower of Christ/ people.

4. Revelation 15:1–16:21

there is a final pouring out of wrath.

As You Finish This Unit . . .

Take a moment now to ask for the Lord's blessing and help as you continue in this study of Revelation. And take a moment also to look back through this unit of study, to reflect on some key things that the Lord may be teaching you—and perhaps to highlight and underline these things to review again in the future.

Definitions

[1] **Benediction** – a prayer for God's blessing at the end of a letter or a worship service. Many NT letters include a benediction.

[2] **Holiness** – a quality possessed by something or someone set apart for special use. When applied to God, it refers to his utter perfection and complete transcendence over creation. God's people are called to imitate his holiness (Lev. 19:2), which means being set apart from sin and reserved for his purposes.

Week 8: The Judgment of God's Enemies, Part 1

Revelation 17:1–19:21

The Place of the Passage

Babylon's fall has already been announced by an angel (14:8) and depicted in the seventh trumpet (16:19). Now, the destruction of this enemy of God is given extensive treatment. We see Babylon symbolized as a prostitute (17:1–6), followed by an angel's explanation of that vision (17:7–18) and then various reactions to Babylon's fall (18:1 – 19:10). Finally, Jesus' final victory over his enemies is seen and celebrated (19:11–21).

The Big Picture

In the end, God's enemies always lose. That is demonstrated to be the case in 17:1–19:21, where the fall of Babylon—and the reaction to that fall (on earth and in heaven)—is vividly depicted.

> ### Reflection and Discussion

Read through the complete passage for this study, Revelation 17:1–19:21. Then write your notes on the following questions. (For further background, see the *ESV Study Bible*, pages 2486–2492, or visit esv.org.)

Revelation 17:1–18 is a description of Babylon and the earthly powers that sustain it. Read verses 1–2, 4–6, and 18. Based on these verses, what do you think the figure of Babylon symbolizes?

Revelation 17:1–2 and 4–6 describe an alluring prostitute arrayed in expensive finery. The "kings of the earth have committed sexual immorality" with her (v. 2). It seems from this description that "Babylon" symbolizes the social, cultural, and economic institutions of human societies that pursue pleasure, luxury, and success apart from God. In John's day, the seductive appeal of godless society was most clearly seen in the "great city" of Rome (17:18). How might Roman society have tempted and seduced the Christians John knew (see Rev. 2:20)? In what ways does godless society tempt modern Christians?

Why is the prostitute sitting on a "scarlet beast"? Who is this beast with seven heads and 10 horns? Compare 17:8 with the description in Revelation 13 of the beast who rises from the sea and is healed from a mortal wound. As in chapter 13, the beast likely represents the power of godless state governments (note that in 17:9–10 the seven heads represent seven kings and in 17:12 the 10 horns represent 10 kings). The Roman empire and its army (the beast) sustains the corrupt and pleasure-seeking ways of the "great city" of Rome (the prostitute). That's still the pattern in our day: governments and armies and economic systems sustain the self-seeking corruption of societies.

The details concerning the prostitute and the beast in 17:7–18 are difficult to understand, and have therefore produced varying interpretations. However, it is clear in these verses that the Lamb conquers his enemies (v. 14) and Babylon falls (vv. 16–18). Surprisingly, it is the beast who (operating under God's sovereign will) destroys the prostitute: the state system that supports the pursuit of godless pleasure will eventually destroy itself. How do these verses remind and reassure Christians that God is in ultimate control?

How do the angelic inhabitants of heaven announce and describe the fall of Babylon in 18:1–8, 21–24? In what ways do they highlight the *severity* of God's judgment on Babylon? In verses 6–8, the voice addresses those who are to carry out God's judgment on Babylon. How are they instructed to proceed? On the basis of these terrible judgments, what are God's people exhorted to do (see vv. 4–5)?

Sandwiched in between the angelic perspectives, we see earthly perspectives on Babylon's fall, in verses 9–20. How do human kings (vv. 9–10), merchants

(vv. 11–17), and shipmasters and sailors (vv. 17–20) respond? Why? How has the prostitute seduced them? How have they profited from godless society's reckless pursuit of pleasure?

We return to the heavenly perspective in Revelation 19. This is no longer reporting or mourning—instead, it is an explosion of exuberant praise (vv. 1–5). For what reasons is God praised here? Is it morally acceptable for the heavenly multitude to praise God for crushing his enemies—is such praise vindictive and unloving? Notice in verses 6–10 that the praise now flows to God not so much for crushing the prostitute as for the great marriage between the Lamb and his "bright and pure" bride. There's a remarkable contrast here between the polluted prostitute and the lovely bride, between the drunk orgies of that prostitute (18:3) and the wedding feast of the Lamb and his bride (19:9).

Revelation 19:11–21 contains an awesome description of the conquering Christ (vv. 11–16), followed by a description of his triumph over the beast, the false prophet, and their followers (vv. 17–21). What becomes of the enemies of Christ? Note the terrible contrast between the wedding feast of the Lamb (v. 9) and the macabre "great supper of God" (vv. 17–18).

Read through the following three sections on *Gospel Glimpses, Whole-Bible Connections,* and *Theological Soundings.* Then take time to consider the *Personal Implications* these sections may have for you.

Gospel Glimpses

THE MARRIAGE SUPPER OF THE LAMB. Revelation 19:7–9 highlights the great marriage supper of the Lamb, a beautiful picture of Jesus' intimate fellowship with his people in the new creation. God's people are depicted as Jesus' bride, clothed "with fine linen, bright and pure," representing "the righteous deeds of the saints" (v. 8). The active involvement of God's people in living holy lives is demonstrated by the assertion that the bride "has made herself ready" (v. 7). God's sovereign grace, which undergirds their activity, is demonstrated by the claim that "it was granted [the bride] to clothe herself with fine linen" (v. 8). It was granted *by God* (for this relationship between God's sovereignty and human responsibility, see Phil. 2:12–13).

GOD'S SWIFT JUDGMENT. God is patient in bringing judgment (2 Pet. 3:9). But when he finally does so, it comes quickly. The swiftness of God's judgment against his enemies is acknowledged by both God's servants (Rev. 18:8) and his enemies (vv. 10, 17, 19). God's victory comes in a "single day," or a "single hour." This demonstrates God's great power (see v. 8), because his enemies are no match for him. Their present success is not because of any weakness or deficiency on his part. It is simply not yet time for his judgment to fall. Revelation 19:1–5 demonstrates that God's great power and swift judgments are reasons for his people to *praise* him.

Whole-Bible Connections

IDOLATRY AND IMMORALITY. Babylon (Rome) is symbolized as a prostitute, and this depiction is in keeping with the Old Testament prophets, who often described idolatry[1] in terms of sexual immorality. Isaiah mourned that Jerusalem had become a prostitute (Isa. 1:21), and Jeremiah spoke of Israel's adulteries (Jer. 2:24). The pagan nations were also described as prostitutes (see Isa. 23:16–17; Nah. 3:4). In the New Testament, James sounds a similar note: "You adulterous people! Do you not know that friendship with the world is enmity with God?" (James 4:4). This linking of idolatry and immorality vividly communicates the uncleanness and spiritual ruin caused by worshiping false gods, as well as the betrayal of God that results.

COME OUT OF HER, MY PEOPLE. John's vision of the prostitute shows that the gravest danger for God's people is often not external persecution but the allurement of prosperity, social advancement, and ease of lifestyle. The carrot may be more dangerous than the stick. The recipients of Revelation were facing both persecution (Rev. 2:10, 13) and enticement (vv. 14, 20), just as God's people in the Old Testament did (see, e.g., the book of Daniel). Jeremiah exhorted Israel to seek the peace of the city where they were sent into exile (Jer. 29:7), but also to get out of Babylon when the opportunity became available (51:45). In Revelation, Christians are not required to physically leave their cities because of the evil done there (Rev. 2:13), but the churches are exhorted to remove worldliness from their midst (vv. 2, 6, 14–16, 20; 18:4). This accords with the teaching of Jesus (John 17:14–15) and Paul (1 Cor. 5:9–13).

A TERRIBLE FEAST. The feast of the marriage supper of the Lamb (Rev. 19:7–9) has a dark counterpart in verses 17–21: "the great supper of God." At this feast, the flesh of God's enemies and their horses is on the menu, and the dinner guests are the carrion birds flying overhead. The guests gorge themselves (v. 21). This terrible vision has deep Old Testament roots. Already in the covenant curses of Deuteronomy, Israel is told that if they disobey, "your dead body shall be food for all birds of the air and for the beasts of the earth" (Deut. 28:26). In Ezekiel 39:4, 17–20 God announced the defeat of Gog and Magog by saying he would give their flesh as food to the birds. The important point made through this terrible image and its Old Testament background is that God will make known his holiness and glory by defeating his enemies (see Ezek. 39:7, 21–25).

Theological Soundings

GOD'S SOVEREIGNTY OVER EVIL. Throughout Revelation, we have seen many affirmations of the sovereignty of God, including his control over the persecution of his own people. The Lamb himself opens the seals in Revelation 6; God "permits" the forces of evil to take peace from the earth; and God "gives authority" to Death and Hades. We see God's sovereignty over evil once again in 17:17. The 10 horns and the beast destroy the prostitute, "for God has put it into their hearts to carry out his purpose." How does God's sovereignty accord with the clear responsibility of Satan and his servants for the evil they do in persecuting God's people (e.g., 6:10–11)? The rest of the New Testament also holds these truths together. In fact, the book of Acts makes clear that humans were responsible for the crucifixion[2] of Jesus, yet also affirms that God ordained even this most evil act of history for good purposes (Acts 2:23; 4:24–28).

IS IT RIGHT TO REJOICE AT GOD'S JUDGMENT? In 19:1–3, God is praised by his people because "he has judged the great prostitute" and because "the smoke from [the prostitute] goes up forever and ever." Is this praise vindictive and immoral? No. God's people rejoice ultimately in God's perfect character, and in the vindication of his character through his just judgments. An unanswered question has hovered over most of Revelation: "O Sovereign Lord, holy and true, how long before you will judge and avenge our blood on those who dwell on the earth?" (6:10). Here in Revelation 19, God's people rejoice that he has responded with perfect righteousness.

Personal Implications

Take time to reflect on the implications of Revelation 17:1–19:21 for your own life today. Consider what you have learned that might lead you to praise God, repent of sin, and trust more deeply in his gracious promises. Make notes below on the personal implications for your walk with the Lord of the (1) *Gospel Glimpses*, (2) *Whole-Bible Connections*, (3) *Theological Soundings*, and (4) this passage as a whole.

1. Gospel Glimpses

2. Whole-Bible Connections

3. Theological Soundings

4. Revelation 17:1–19:21

> ### As You Finish This Unit . . .

Take a moment now to ask for the Lord's blessing and help as you continue in this study of Revelation. And take a moment also to look back through this unit of study, to reflect on some key things that the Lord may be teaching you—and perhaps to highlight and underline these things to review again in the future.

Definitions

[1] **Idolatry** – in the Bible usually refers to the worship of a physical object. Paul's comments in Colossians 3:5, however, indicate that idolatry can include covetousness, since it is essentially equivalent to worshiping material things.

[2] **Crucifixion** – means of execution in which the person was fastened, by ropes or nails, to a crossbeam that was then raised and attached to a vertical beam, forming a cross (the root meaning of "crucifixion"). The process was designed to maximize pain and humiliation, and to serve as a deterrent for other potential offenders. Jesus suffered this form of execution (Matt. 27:32–56), not for any offense he had committed (Heb. 4:15) but as the atoning sacrifice for all who would believe in him (John 3:16).

WEEK 9: THE JUDGMENT
OF GOD'S ENEMIES, PART 2

Revelation 20:1–15

The Place of the Passage

Thus far in Revelation, John has seen visions that depict the events of this present age between the two comings of Jesus, with occasional "fast-forwards" to the end-time events of the final judgment and the new creation. This pattern of moving from the present age to the end-time future, back to the present, back to the future, and so forth, is called "recapitulation," and is found in Daniel and other Old Testament prophets. The same pattern continues in Revelation 20:1–15, as John once again sees the realities of this present age, followed by the final defeat of Satan and the final judgment.

The Big Picture

Revelation 20:1–15 depicts the realities of this present age, followed by a picture of the final judgment of Satan and all his followers.

▶ **Reflection and Discussion**

Read through the complete passage for this study, Revelation 20:1–15. Then review the shorter passages below and write your own notes on the following questions. (For further background, see the *ESV Study Bible*, pages 2492–2493, or visit esv.org.)

1. Satan (20:1–10)

We have seen already in 9:1 that God owns the key to the bottomless pit: he has ultimate authority over it, but he has given Satan limited control. God's authority is confirmed here in 20:1, as we see an angel coming down from heaven, holding the key in his hand. The angel seizes Satan and binds him "for a thousand years," throwing him into the pit and shutting and sealing it over him. The purpose of this confinement is "so that [Satan] might not deceive the nations any longer, until the thousand years were ended. After that he must be released for a little while" (v. 3). Opinions regarding the meaning of 20:1–3 diverge sharply. To take two of the main views, premillennialists understand the "thousand years" to refer to a future, millennial kingdom in which Jesus reigns on earth, while amillennialists believe the "thousand years" refers to the entire present age between the first and second comings of Jesus. According to a premillennial understanding of 20:2–3, the binding and sealing of Satan represents God's complete removal of Satan from the earth during the future millennial reign of Christ. Amillennialists, however, see the binding of Satan as a restraint of his deceptive activity during the present age, a restraint that allows the spread of the gospel among the nations.

Read Matthew 12:22–32. According to this passage (especially v. 29), at what point was Satan bound? How might this help us to understand the binding of Satan "for a thousand years" in Revelation 20:2? In what ways is Satan's deception of the nations restricted during this present age? In what ways will Satan's deception increase at the end of this age (compare 20:3, 7–8 with 16:12–16)?

Again, opinions about 20:4–6 diverge. Premillennialists understand these verses to describe the future millennial reign of Christ and his people on earth before the final judgment and the new creation. On this view, "they came to life" (20:4) refers to the bodily resurrection[1] of believers. Amillennialists, on the other hand, understand this passage to describe the present reign (see 20:6) of God's people in heaven, not on earth. The one thousand years is interpreted symbolically, referring to a long period of time. On this view, "they came to life" refers (ironically) to the saints' physical death, which leads to spiritual life in heaven, where they presently reign with Christ. The rest of the dead, those who died apart from Christ, "did not come to life"; they await physical resurrection at the end of the age. What strengths and weaknesses do you see in these views?

Revelation 20:6 contains the fifth of Revelation's seven benedictions. God's blessing is granted to the one who shares in "the first resurrection," that is, life in heaven with Christ. The "second death," that is, eternal death in the lake of fire (see 20:14), has no power over Christ's followers.

In 20:7–10, we witness the total defeat of Satan. The final battle, mentioned already in 16:13–16 and 19:17–21, is described here once again, and this time Satan's final defeat is emphasized (20:10). What clues in these verses make clear that this victory belongs to God?

2. Unbelievers (20:11–15)

Already in 6:12–17 and 11:18, we've caught glimpses of the final judgment. Here in 20:11–15 we see it described yet more fully. How does the color of God's throne and the response of earth and sky emphasize his perfect holiness and power?

In what ways does 20:12–15 emphasize the comprehensive nature of the final judgment?

What is meant by saying that "Death and Hades were thrown into the lake of fire"?

Which books are opened before God's throne? What is written in these books? What do you think is the difference between the "books" and the "book of life"?

Read through the following three sections on *Gospel Glimpses*, *Whole-Bible Connections*, and *Theological Soundings*. Then take time to consider the *Personal Implications* these sections may have for you.

▶ Gospel Glimpses

THE BOOKS AND THE BOOK. In 20:11–15, the "books" contain the deeds of every person (vv. 12–13). The "book of life" contains the names of those for whom Christ died (compare 3:5; 17:8; 20:15). In 13:8, this book is called "the book of life of the Lamb who was slain," and in 21:27, "the Lamb's book of life," emphasizing that those written in it are recipients of all the benefits of Christ's work on the cross. They are, moreover, recipients of that work through God's grace alone, since their names have been written in it from before the foundation of the world (13:8; 17:8). This distinction between the "books" and the "book of life" shows that unbelievers are condemned on the basis of their deeds, while God's people are saved through Christ's redemptive work, not their deeds. Instead, their deeds confirm the reality of their trust in Christ and his completed work on their behalf. Salvation is by grace through faith alone.

▶ Whole-Bible Connections

REVERSING THE CURSE. When Adam and Eve sinned, death entered the world (see Gen. 2:17; Rom. 5:12). Revelation 20:11–15 demonstrates God's final triumph over death, for those whose names have been written in the book of life will not *remain* physically dead, but will live forever in the new creation (see 21:27). Death is destroyed (20:14) through the death of Jesus on the cross—the book of life is called "the book of life of the Lamb who was slain" (13:8). This agrees with what Paul writes: "For as by a man came death, by a man has come also the resurrection of the dead. For as in Adam all die, so also in Christ shall all be made alive. . . . The last enemy to be destroyed is death" (1 Cor. 15:21–22, 26).

REIGNING WITH CHRIST. Already in Revelation 1:6, Christ's death is said to have freed believers from their sins and made them "a kingdom" and priests. As we've seen, this recalls the promise God gave Israel that they would be a "kingdom of priests and a holy nation" (Ex. 19:6). Israel's role as a kingdom of priests,[2] in turn, recalls Adam's royal function in the garden of Eden, where he was created in the "image of God" (language used of a king in the ancient Near Eastern context) and commissioned to "fill the earth and subdue it, and have dominion over" it (Gen. 1:27–28). Moreover, Adam's responsibility in the garden was to "work it and keep it" (2:15), terms used for the work of Israel's priests (Num. 3:7–8). Adam was a priest and a king. Israel was to be a kingdom of priests. Now, through Christ's redemptive work, God's people are given this commission. They will serve as priests forever (Rev. 7:15) and will reign as kings forever (3:21; 22:5). In Revelation 20:6, we see that already in this age, those who die in Christ are given the responsibility of reigning with him and serving as priests. Humans are freed through Christ to fulfill the glorious responsibility first intended for Adam.

Theological Soundings

SATAN IS NO MATCH FOR GOD. Throughout Revelation, we've seen that Satan is not the equal-and-opposite of God but instead is infinitely less powerful. That is emphasized once again in Revelation 20:1–10, in several ways. First, an angelic messenger comes from heaven, holding the key to the bottomless pit. This reminds us that God, not Satan, is in ultimate control of the pit. Second, the angel of God is powerful enough to seize and bind Satan; if even God's servant is more powerful than Satan, God must be much more powerful. Third, Satan can leave the pit only when he is "released" (vv. 3, 7) by God. Fourth, the devil suffers a decisive, final, eternal defeat: with no hint of struggle, he is "thrown into the lake of fire and sulfur" and "tormented day and night forever and ever" (v. 10). Satan has the great advantages of longevity (he is the "ancient" serpent in v. 2) and an ability to deceive (v. 8). But he is no match for God. That must have been a major encouragement to the original readers of Revelation, who were suffering Satan's attacks (see 2:9, 13; 3:8–9). It can be an equally precious reminder to modern readers.

Personal Implications

Take time to reflect on the implications of Revelation 20:1–15 for your own life today. Consider what you have learned that might lead you to praise God, repent of sin, and trust more deeply in his gracious promises. Make notes below on the personal implications for your walk with the Lord of the (1) *Gospel Glimpses*, (2) *Whole-Bible Connections*, (3) *Theological Soundings*, and (4) this passage as a whole.

1. Gospel Glimpses

2. Whole-Bible Connections

3. Theological Soundings

4. Revelation 20:1–15

As You Finish This Unit . . .

Take a moment now to ask for the Lord's blessing and help as you continue in this study of Revelation. And take a moment also to look back through this unit of study, to reflect on some key things that the Lord may be teaching you—and perhaps to highlight and underline these things to review again in the future.

Definitions

[1] **Resurrection** – the impartation of new, eternal physical life to a dead person at the end of time (or in the case of Jesus, on the third day after his death). This new life is not a mere resuscitation of the body (as in the case of Lazarus; John 11:1–44) but a transformation of the body to an eternal state (1 Cor. 15:35–58). Both the righteous and the wicked will be resurrected, the former to eternal life and the latter to judgment (John 5:29)

[2] **Priest** – In OT Israel, the priest represented the people before God, and God before the people. Only those descended from Aaron could be priests. Their prescribed duties also included inspecting and receiving sacrifices from the people and overseeing the daily activities and maintenance of the tabernacle or temple.

WEEK 10: GOD'S PEOPLE PERFECT IN GLORY

Revelation 21:1–22:5

▲

Revelation is a book on tiptoe, leaning forward to the new creation. Already in chapters 2–3, we're repeatedly pointed to the ultimate future, with references to the tree of life in the paradise of God (2:7); the new Jerusalem (3:12); and the prospect of reigning forever with Christ (3:21). Revelation 7:15–17 provides another flash-forward glimpse of the new creation (see also 14:1–5), and therefore bears striking similarities to 21:1–22:5 (e.g., the promise of God "tabernacling" with his people, the hardships of life passing away, Jesus giving living water, and God wiping away every tear). Now, in 21:1–22:5, we get our longest and richest look at the eternal future of God's people—a prospect that must have been enormously encouraging to struggling first-century Christians and is also hope-giving for twenty-first-century Christians.

The Big Picture

Revelation 21:1–22:5 offers a breathtaking view of the eternal future of God's people.

Reflection and Discussion

Read through the complete passage for this study, Revelation 21:1–22:5. Then write your notes on the following questions. (For further background, see the *ESV Study Bible*, pages 2494–2496, or visit esv.org.)

In our passage, John provides a stunning description of God's new heaven and new earth. Read 21:1. Do you think God's new creation is completely new, a total replacement of this current world? Remembering that any given portion of Scripture must be interpreted in light of the rest of Scripture, read Romans 8:20–21. Does this passage shed light on the question? Compare 1 Corinthians 15:35–44 for help in thinking through the related question of the differences and similarities between our present bodies and our future, resurrection bodies. What are your conclusions?

In John's vision of the new creation, the "sea was no more" (Rev. 21:1). Does that mean there will be no more bodies of water in the new creation? Read 22:1–2. Now read Daniel 7:3 and Revelation 13:1. Given these passages, what do you think the sea in 21:1 represents? Therefore, what will be completely absent in the new creation?

How is the *beauty* of God's new creation emphasized in John's vision (see, for example, 21:2, 11, 18–21; 22:1–5)?

The description of God's new creation and God's new people in 21:1–22:5 shows the blessings we will enjoy as gifts from God. Take a moment to identify the blessings mentioned in these verses. As you do this, note that the most terrible things in life will be gone forever (e.g., 21:4). Note also the safety and security represented by the great wall around the new Jerusalem (21:12); the presence of abundant material wealth everywhere (21:18–21); and the eternal life enjoyed by all (22:1–2).

The lavish descriptions of blessing in 21:1–22:5 make clear that the main reason the new creation is amazing is that *God himself* will be present with his people. Take time to note all the ways this point is made:

What words/images are used to describe God's relationship with his people (21:2, 3, 7, 9; 22:3)? How do these convey intimacy and belonging?

The Greek words for "dwelling place" and "dwell" in 21:3 are the same as the word for the "tabernacle" in the Old Testament (compare John 1:14). How does the use of this word "tabernacle" emphasize the theme of God's presence?

How is the truth of God's perfect presence emphasized in the description of the new Jerusalem? Note especially the dimensions of the city (21:16), as well as its construction of pure gold (21:18). Compare this with 1 Kings 6:20. What point is being made here? In light of the elaborate requirements necessary for the high priest to enter the Most Holy Place only *once a year* (see Leviticus 16), how privileged are those who live in the new creation?

Note also in Revelation 22:4 that God's people "will see his face." Reflect on the significance of this promise in light of Exodus 33:20–23; 34:29–35.

One of the angels with the seven bowls beckons John to come so that he can show him the "Bride, the wife of the Lamb" (Rev. 21:9). Note the similar phrasing in 17:1, where the angel shows John another woman—in that instance,

Babylon the prostitute. Compare and contrast the prostitute and the bride. Why do you think they are juxtaposed over against each other in this way?

What is the significance of the 12 names written on the gates (21:12) and the 12 names written on the foundations of the wall (v. 14) of the new Jerusalem?

What hints do you see in 21:1–22:5 that this new creation is *even better* than Eden?

Read through the following three sections on *Gospel Glimpses*, *Whole-Bible Connections*, and *Theological Soundings*. Then take time to consider the *Personal Implications* these sections may have for you.

Gospel Glimpses

WATER WITHOUT PAYMENT. Revelation 21:8 makes clear that sinful deeds for which there is no repentance (compare 16:9, 11, 21) prohibit one from entering the new creation. But the book of Revelation is equally clear that good deeds cannot earn one's way into heaven—rather, the blood of the Lamb is required for forgiveness of sin (Rev. 1:5). God offers a beautiful gospel promise in Revelation 21:6: "To the thirsty I will give from the spring of the water of life without payment" (compare 22:17). Three words underscore the amazing grace of God. First, God says he will "give" from the spring of the water of life. Second, he says he will give this water "without payment." Third, the requirement for receiving this gift has nothing to do with being able to pay God back. God says he will give the water to the "thirsty," that is, those who know they need the water, and want it very badly. This promise of free water is the free offer of the gospel, and recalls the words of Isaiah 55:1: "Come, everyone who thirsts, come to the waters; and he who has no money, come, buy and eat! Come, buy wine and milk without money and without price."

▶ Whole-Bible Connections

NO MORE SEA. Revelation 21:1 asserts that in the new creation, "the sea was no more." This draws on a long association in the Old Testament between the sea and the forces of chaos, rebellion, and danger (see, e.g., Isa. 57:20). In Daniel 7:3, four beasts come up out of the sea; and in Revelation 13:1, the beast rises out of the sea. The absence of the sea in the new creation does not mean there will be no bodies of water; rather, it means that the enemies of God associated with the sea will be no more. Note the verbal parallels between Revelation 21:1 and 21:4: "the sea was no more"; "death shall be no more, neither shall there be mourning, nor crying, nor pain anymore."

THE TABERNACLE AND THE MOST HOLY PLACE. The tabernacle, a moveable tent that accompanied Israel through its wilderness wanderings, was very important in Israel's history. Somewhat ironically, the separating of a holy God *from* his sinful people allowed God to live *among* his people. The tabernacle was a place of sacrifice and feasting and joy, a place to which God's people longed to return when they were far away (see Ps. 63:1–2). So, it is significant that Revelation 21:3 twice uses the word for "tabernacle": "Behold, the dwelling place ["tabernacle"] of God is with man. He will dwell ["tabernacle"] with them" (see the ESV textual footnote). By calling to mind the tabernacle, God is assuring his people that they will enjoy his presence in the new creation. This promise is heightened in 21:15–21, where the new Jerusalem is pictured as a perfect cube (21:16) made of pure gold (21:18, 21). That striking description calls to mind the Most Holy Place of the temple (1 Kings 6:20). God's people will live in God's perfect presence forever, an amazing privilege. They will see his face (Rev. 22:4), a privilege not even Moses enjoyed. There will be no need for the temple (21:22), because God's people will enjoy his perfect presence forever.

RETURNED TO GOD'S PRESENCE. Adam and Eve were originally permitted to live in God's presence in the garden of Eden but were "exiled" from the garden after they sinned (Genesis 3). Similarly, the nation of Israel was chosen to be the place of God's presence, with the tabernacle and later the temple, but they too sinned against God. As a result, they were exiled from the Promised Land, and God's glory departed from the temple (Ezekiel 10). Revelation 21–22 highlights the reversal of the curse of separation from God, together with all the death, mourning, crying, and pain it entails (21:4). These chapters describe the new creation, using language reminiscent of Eden (e.g., references to water sources and the tree of life), indicating that finally the effects of the fall will be reversed and God's people will be returned to his presence. Exile will be over. But John's vision suggests that the new creation is even *better* than Eden: there are two trees of life (not one); this paradise lasts forever (rather than ending abruptly with a fall into sin); and the Lamb will be present as the focus of eternal worship (22:3).

Theological Soundings

THE PEOPLE OF GOD. Inscribed on the gates of the new Jerusalem are the names of the 12 tribes of the sons of Israel (21:12). On the 12 foundations of the city wall are written the names of the 12 apostles of the Lamb (21:14). This symbolizes the profound unity of God's new covenant people, all of whom are equally and fully part of God's people through the blood of the Lamb (1:5). God's purpose for Jews and Gentiles was that Christ would "create in himself one new man in place of the two, so making peace, and might reconcile us both to God in one body through the cross, thereby killing the hostility" (Eph. 2:15–16). Revelation 21 shows this purpose fully and gloriously realized.

Personal Implications

Take time to reflect on the implications of Revelation 21:1–22:5 for your own life today. Consider what you have learned that might lead you to praise God, repent of sin, and trust more deeply in his gracious promises. Make notes below on the personal implications for your walk with the Lord of the (1) *Gospel Glimpses*, (2) *Whole-Bible Connections*, (3) *Theological Soundings*, and (4) this passage as a whole.

1. Gospel Glimpses

2. Whole-Bible Connections

3. Theological Soundings

4. Revelation 21:1–22:5

> ### As You Finish This Unit . . .

Take a moment now to ask for the Lord's blessing and help as you continue in this study of Revelation. And take a moment also to look back through this unit of study, to reflect on some key things that the Lord may be teaching you—and perhaps to highlight and underline these things to review again in the future.

WEEK 11: EPILOGUE

Revelation 22:6–21

▲

The epilogue of Revelation (22:6–21) forms a clear bookend with the prologue (1:1–8). Both emphasize the trustworthiness of this revelation from God, and also the chain of transmission by which it comes from God to his people (1:1–4; 22:6, 8–9, 16). Both highlight the blessedness of those who hear and keep the words of this book (1:3; 22:7). In the prologue, God identifies himself as the Alpha and Omega (1:8); in the epilogue, Jesus identifies himself as "the Alpha and the Omega, the first and the last, the beginning and the end" (22:13). Both the prologue and the epilogue emphasize that the things recorded in the book "must soon take place" (1:1; 22:6), that "the time is near" (1:3; 22:10), and that Jesus "is coming soon" (22:7, 12, 20).

The Big Picture

The epilogue of Revelation emphasizes once again the complete trustworthiness of this book and the divine blessing for those who hear and keep it.

> ## Reflection and Discussion

Read through the complete passage for this study, Revelation 22:6–21. Then write your notes on the following questions. (For further background, see the *ESV Study Bible*, pages 2496–2497, or visit esv.org.)

Read Revelation 22:6. Why "must" these things soon take place? Recall the same word "must" in 1:1. What is the significance of this word, and why would it have been so comforting to the original readers? How have we seen God's sovereign power and plan emphasized throughout Revelation?

In 22:7, Jesus says, "I am coming soon" (also vv. 12, 20; see also vv. 6, 10). But it's now been about two thousand years (and counting). Was Jesus wrong?

Revelation 22:7 pronounces a divine blessing on "the one who keeps the words of the prophecy of this book." Having now read all the way through the book of Revelation, what do you think it means to "keep" the words of this book? Are you experiencing this blessing?

Compare 19:10 and 22:8–9. John makes the same mistake twice, in rapid succession! Why? How is he reproved and corrected?

Why do you think Jesus says, in 22:11, "Let the evildoer still do evil, and the filthy still be filthy, and the righteous still do right, and the holy still be holy"? Is he encouraging sin? Doesn't he want repentance?

What does 22:14–15 teach about how a person can enjoy access to the new creation? What does it teach about what excludes a person from the new creation?

While the epilogue of Revelation closely parallels the prologue, the strong warning of 22:18–19 is unique. Note the divine justice accorded those who "add" to the words of the book—God will "add" to him the plagues described in this book (v. 18). What plagues are described in Revelation? Divine justice is enacted negatively as well—"if anyone takes away from the words of the book of this prophecy, God will take away his share in the tree of life and in the holy city" (v. 19). What is at stake when it comes to tampering with the book of Revelation? Why are the consequences so drastic?

Read through the following three sections on *Gospel Glimpses, Whole-Bible Connections,* and *Theological Soundings.* Then take time to consider the *Personal Implications* these sections may have for you.

▶ Gospel Glimpses

THE BOOK OF REVELATION AND DIVINE BLESSING. As we have seen in our study of Revelation, seven blessings are scattered throughout. The first is in 1:3, where John pronounces a blessing on those who hear and keep the words of this book. In 22:7 we find the penultimate blessing: "Blessed is the one who keeps the words of the prophecy of this book." These bookends make clear that one of the main aims of Revelation is to bring blessing to God's people as they hear and "keep" it. This book is not an apocalyptic puzzle or code to be figured out. Rather, it is a source of divine blessing for God's suffering people as they "keep" the ways it instructs them to live (compare 14:12).

HOW TO ENTER THE GATES. Unrepentant disobedience disqualifies a person from the new creation (21:8; 22:15). But, as we've already seen, it is not by one's own obedience that one enters the gates of the new Jerusalem. Rather, it is washing one's robes (22:14) that gives one the right to the tree of life. Comparing 22:15 with Revelation 7:14 is illuminating: "They have washed their robes and made them white in the blood of the Lamb" (7:14). It is the cleansing, sin-bearing death of Jesus on the cross that allows his people salvation and therefore access to the new creation. Obedience to the commands of Christ flows from trusting in him and his sin-bearing work.

ENDING ON TIPTOE. The book of Revelation consistently points toward the eternal future, moving back and forth from the realities of this present age to tantalizing visions of the age to come, in which God will recreate the earth and be perfectly present with his people. The key transition to that age is the coming of Jesus. And so the book ends on tiptoe, yearning for his future coming: "He who testifies to these things says, 'Surely I am coming soon.' Amen. Come, Lord Jesus!" (22:20). This is the cry of the early church: "Maranatha! Our Lord, come!" (compare 1 Cor. 16:22). In the meantime, God's people are promised the grace of the Lord Jesus, the one who walks among the lampstands, who will aid them in their present struggles until he returns (Rev. 22:21).

▶ Whole-Bible Connections

THE ROOT AND DESCENDANT OF DAVID. In 22:16, Jesus identifies himself as "the root and the descendant of David, the bright morning star." This remarkable self-identification points toward Jesus' messianic status and, further, toward his deity.[1] Jesus is the ultimate fulfillment of God's ancient promises of a coming king, a promise that goes all the way back to Genesis, where God told Abraham, "I will make you exceedingly fruitful, and I will make you into nations, and kings shall come from you" (Gen. 17:6). This royal promise was later renewed to Jacob (35:11) and Judah (49:10), and fulfilled in part through David and his son Solomon. But even in David's day there was a promise of a greater son (2 Samuel 7). Isaiah spoke of a coming one, "a shoot from the stump of Jesse, and a branch from his roots" (Isa. 11:1). He would be both David's offspring and his Lord (compare Psalm 110 and Mark 12:35–37). As the Lion of the tribe of Judah and the Root of David (Rev. 5:5), Jesus Christ is the ultimate fulfillment of this promise. Even though he is David's descendant (Matt. 1:17), he *precedes* and surpasses David. He is more than a human king. He shares in God's sovereign rule and throne (Rev. 22:1).

▶ Theological Soundings

THE DEITY OF CHRIST. When John falls down to worship at the feet of the angel who shows him the vision, the response of the angel is unequivocal: "You must not do that! I am a fellow servant with you and your brothers the prophets, and with those who keep the words of this book. Worship God" (Rev. 22:9). This isn't John's first mistake, nor the angel's first strong correction (see 19:10). There is clearly an absolute dividing line between God and his messengers: God is to be worshiped, but not his angels. It is striking, therefore, that when John falls down at the feet of Jesus (1:17), he is *not* reproved for doing so. In fact, Jesus responds by affirming his eternal being in terms normally reserved for God himself. Jesus is rightly to be worshiped (compare 5:8–14).

THE TIME IS NEAR. The prologue asserted that the revelation of Jesus "must *soon* take place" (1:1) because "the time is near" (1:3). These claims are repeated in the epilogue: John is shown what "must soon take place" (22:6); Jesus is coming soon (22:7, 12, 20); and "the time is near" (22:10). How could John properly make these claims, since two thousand years have now elapsed since the writing of Revelation? It is important to recall that the book of Revelation, together with the rest of the New Testament, understands the first coming of Jesus to have begun the last days. Most of the end-time events prophesied throughout Revelation receive at least a beginning fulfillment in the period in which John is writing (and in our own day as well). This is true even of Jesus' promise that he is coming soon. Although the focus of his words is clearly his public, end-time return, probably also included are his comings throughout the present age, prior to his final return (e.g., 2:5).

Personal Implications

Take time to reflect on the implications of Revelation 22:6–21 for your own life today. Consider what you have learned that might lead you to praise God, repent of sin, and trust more deeply in his gracious promises. Make notes below on the personal implications for your walk with the Lord of the (1) *Gospel Glimpses*, (2) *Whole-Bible Connections*, (3) *Theological Soundings*, and (4) this passage as a whole.

1. Gospel Glimpses

2. Whole-Bible Connections

3. Theological Soundings

4. Revelation 22:6–21

As You Finish This Unit . . .

Take a moment now to ask for the Lord's blessing and help as you continue in this study of Revelation. And take a moment also to look back through this unit of study, to reflect on some key things that the Lord may be teaching you—and perhaps to highlight and underline these things to review again in the future.

Definitions

[1] **Deity** – God's unique, essential nature as supreme and eternal. Jesus, the Son of God, possesses deity. He is fully God, as is the Holy Spirit.

Week 12: Summary and Conclusion

▲

As we draw our study of Revelation to a close, we'll summarize the big picture of God's message throughout the book, and then consider several questions in order to reflect on Gospel Glimpses, Whole-Bible Connections, and Theological Soundings with a view to Revelation as a whole.

The Big Picture of Revelation

We've seen in this study that Revelation begins with a prologue, ends with an epilogue, and has seven main sections in between. It paints a sober, realistic picture of what life will be like for Christ's church in this world; there will be enticing temptations and violent persecutions, and the church will often look insignificant and weak. But because God has a sovereign plan for his people, and because Christ has freed Christians from their sins by his blood (1:5), it is possible for Christians to live victoriously. It's just that victory will not always *look* like victory. Like Christ's triumph at the cross, it will often be an ironic victory; a victory (15:2) that looks like defeat (13:7). Just as the expected conquering Lion of Judah appeared as a slain Lamb (5:5–6), so God's holy army (7:1–8; 14:1–5) will win by losing and dying (12:11). God's people are called to endure (1:9; 13:10; 14:12) in obedience to God and faith in Christ, to be faithful unto death, and then to enjoy eternal life. The churches can be assured that in all the trials and suffering, Christ will be walking among the lampstands (1:13). His grace will be with them (22:21). (For further background, see the *ESV Study Bible*, pages 2453–2462; also online at esv.org.)

Gospel Glimpses

The beautiful, full-orbed gospel of Jesus Christ is on display throughout the book of Revelation. Jesus is the "firstborn of the dead" and the one who "has freed us from our sins by his blood" (1:5). From the word "must" in 1:1 all the way to the same word in 22:6, and throughout the book, we see God unfolding his sovereign, gracious plan. Nothing—not even the suffering of God's people, or the evil acts of God's enemies—happens apart from his sovereign will. God brings blessing to his people (as evident from the sevenfold blessing pronounced throughout Revelation), and his ultimate plan is to renew the entire creation (Revelation 21–22). Grace flows to the readers of the book from the Father, Spirit, and Son (1:4–5). In fact, the entire book ends on a "grace note": "The grace of the Lord Jesus be with all. Amen."

Has this study of the book of Revelation brought new clarity to your understanding of the gospel? How so?

Have there been any particular passages or themes in Revelation that have led you to a fresh grasp of God's grace through Jesus?

> ## Whole-Bible Connections

God's plan in Revelation makes sense only within the larger storyline of Scripture. The task of being God's priest and king, which both Adam and Israel failed to accomplish, is now fulfilled in Christ, who, as the ultimate king in the line of David, and the *root* of David (22:16), reigns triumphantly. The pervasive allusions to the Old Testament throughout the book of Revelation demonstrate that Jesus Christ is the climax and goal of history. Amazingly, Christ not only saves a people for God through his blood (1:5), but then he shares his commission to be a priest and king with his people, both Jew and Gentile, whom he makes to be "a kingdom, priests to his God and Father" (1:6). Furthermore, God creates a perfect place for his new people. The original creation, ruined through Adam's sin, will be renewed by God, made even better than the first creation (chs. 21–22).

How has your understanding of the place of Revelation in the sweep of the Bible been deepened through this study?

What are some connections in Revelation to the Old Testament that you hadn't noticed before?

Were there any themes emphasized in Revelation that have helped deepen your grasp of the Bible's unity?

What development has there been in your view of who Jesus is and how he fulfills the Old Testament?

> ## Theological Soundings

Revelation has much to contribute to Christian theology. Perhaps most important is that it repeatedly affirms the deity of Jesus Christ, who receives the worship due only to the one true God (compare 4:11 and 5:12, and see 5:13–14). Revelation also contains important biblical teaching on the existence and reality of Satan and his demons; the sovereignty of God; the necessity of obedience for final salvation; hell; and the new creation.

Where has your theology been corrected, shaped, deepened, or improved through this study of Revelation?

How might our understanding of God be impoverished if we did not have the book of Revelation?

How does the book of Revelation uniquely contribute to our understanding of Jesus?

Are there specific ways in which Revelation helps us understand what it means to be a faithful Christian?

Personal Implications

As you consider the book of Revelation as a whole, what implications do you see for your own life? Consider especially the issue of what it means to be a faithful, "victorious" Christian in this life.

As You Finish Studying Revelation . . .

We rejoice with you as you finish studying the book of Revelation! May this study become part of your Christian walk of faith, day by day and week by week throughout all your life. Now we would greatly encourage you to study the Word of God on a week-by-week basis. To continue your study of the Bible, we would encourage you to consider other books in the *Knowing the Bible* series, and to visit www.knowingthebibleseries.org.

Lastly, take a moment to look back through this study. Review the notes that you have written, and the things that you have highlighted or underlined. Reflect again on the key themes that the Lord has been teaching you about himself and about his Word. May these things become a treasure for you throughout your life—this we pray in the name of the Father, and the Son, and the Holy Spirit. Amen.

KNOWING THE BIBLE STUDY GUIDE SERIES

Experience the *Grace* of God in the *Word* of God, Book by Book

— Series Volumes —

- Genesis
- Exodus
- Leviticus
- Numbers
- Deuteronomy
- Joshua
- Judges
- Ruth and Esther
- 1–2 Samuel
- 1–2 Kings
- 1–2 Chronicles
- Ezra and Nehemiah
- Job
- Psalms
- Proverbs
- Ecclesiastes
- Song of Solomon

- Isaiah
- Jeremiah
- Lamentations, Habakkuk, and Zephaniah
- Ezekiel
- Daniel
- Hosea
- Joel, Amos, and Obadiah
- Jonah, Micah, and Nahum
- Haggai, Zechariah, and Malachi
- Matthew
- Mark
- Luke

- John
- Acts
- Romans
- 1 Corinthians
- 2 Corinthians
- Galatians
- Ephesians
- Philippians
- Colossians and Philemon
- 1–2 Thessalonians
- 1–2 Timothy and Titus
- Hebrews
- James
- 1–2 Peter and Jude
- 1–3 John
- Revelation

crossway.org/knowingthebible